On the Red Horse, Peter and Paul—
A Small Book about a Big War
(Diary Entries, Articles, Letters, 1991-1998)

O riđanu, Petru i Pavlu—
mala knjiga o velikom ratu
(Dnevnički zapisi, članci, pisma, 1991.-1998.)

On the Red Horse, Peter and Paul— A Small Book about a Big War (Diary Entries, Articles, Letters, 1991-1998)

O riđanu, Petru i Pavlu— mala knjiga o velikom ratu (Dnevnički zapisi, članci, pisma, 1991.-1998.)

By

Helena Peričić

Translated by Petra Sapun and Proofread by Nick Saywell

CAMBRIDGE
SCHOLARS
PUBLISHING

On the Red Horse, Peter and Paul—A Small Book about a Big War
(Diary Entries, Articles, Letters, 1991-1998)
O riđanu, Petru i Pavlu—mala knjiga o velikom ratu
(Dnevnički zapisi, članci, pisma, 1991.-1998.),
by Helena Peričić

This book first published 2010

Cambridge Scholars Publishing

12 Back Chapman Street, Newcastle upon Tyne, NE6 2XX, UK

British Library Cataloguing in Publication Data
A catalogue record for this book is available from the British Library

ISBN (10): 1-4438-1766-X, ISBN (13): 978-1-4438-1766-0

The translation of this book was financially supported by:
City of Zadar
County of Zadar

To Ema
(Un)forgivably sincerely

Emi
(ne)oprostivo iskreno

So many have been shot that a person can easily get lost in this cemetery. Generally speaking, it is hard to tell who killed whom. Those who killed yesterday are gone today. The same as the ones that they killed, and those who will do the killing tomorrow; they too will be gone tomorrow, and those who will shoot and hang tomorrow won't have any idea that we, today, are the ones they've killed and burned at the stake. Generally speaking, it is hard to know who killed whom and why, and who is still alive and who is dead—

—From Miroslav Krleža's *Aretej*[1]

Tolike su postrijeljali da se čovjek ne snalazi na ovom groblju. Uopće: teško je znati tko je koga ubio. Oni koji su ubijali jučer, tih više nema, upravo kao ni onih koje su pobili, a oni koji ubijaju danas, tih neće biti sutra, a oni koji će i strijeljati ili vješati sutra, ti neće imati pojma kako su ubijali i palili na lomačama nas, danas, i uopće teško je znati tko je koga ubio i zašto, a tko je živ a tko mrtav—

—Iz *Areteja* Miroslava Krleže

[1] Miroslav Krleža, a famous Croatian author (1893-1981)

TABLE OF CONTENTS

FOREWORD

On The Red Horse, Peter and Paul is one of those manuscripts that the author does not want to remember, does not want to check, proofread, or change in any way. Each new reading of a text, in this case a text that stands as a witness to days that are "long gone" but which were survived with great difficulty, presents a reliving of everything that was stated in it.

This is an utterly honest confession consisting of diary entries, published articles or those intended for publication, of texts read on air on radio shows, lyrical fragments, a few stories, letters... The manuscript describes events – both on a collective and an individual level – that took place between 1991 and 1998, even though the perspective and comments (stressed in *italics*) date from a later period (1998–2004).

Not a single person mentioned in this manuscript is a work of fiction; some of them close to me no longer live in these parts, I haven't had any contact with others for a long time, some are gone etc., but each of them is a part of this testimony about a time in which I, the author, bear no importance. I believe that this text is relevant as an individual perspective, as one of *many possible* perspectives. Actually, as it happens, this perspective was very often everything I as the author had in those critical situations, situations such as I previously knew only from my childhood textbooks and readers – never even suspecting that I myself would one day go through anything similar.

In that binary system, the only thing that mattered was "whether you were there or not", as I once wrote. I beg of those close to me and whom I mention here to forgive me for dragging them once again, without even asking, into an era that they barely and with difficulty escaped, and which they probably don't even want to remember. By using their real names, I have tried to show that the individuals and their *individual destinies* – were more important than the "collective events" and "the course of the world". I remember these names with tenderness and gratitude.

—The author
Zadar, early July 2004

PREDGOVOR

O riđanu, Petru i Pavlu jedan je od onih rukopisa kojih se autor(ica) ne želi sjećati, koje ne želi provjeravati, ispravljati, revidirati. Naime, svako novo iščitavanje teksta koje u ovom slučaju svjedoči o danima „davno prošlim" a teško preživljenim predstavlja ponovno proživljavanje svega što je u tekstu navedeno.

Ovo je krajnje iskrena ispovijest sastavljena od dnevničkih zapisa, članaka objavljenih ili planiranih za objavljivanje, od tekstova čitanih u radio-emisijama, lirskih zapisa, od pokoje priče, pisama... Rukopis obuhvaća događaje – kako na kolektivnoj tako na individualnoj razini – od 1991. do 1998. iako se javlja (*kurzivom* naglašeno) perspektiva iz nešto kasnijega/kasnijih doba (1998.-2004.).

Niti jedna osoba koja je u ovom rukopisu spomenuta nije izmišljena; neke od njih meni bliskih ne žive više u ovom prostoru, s nekima od njih odavna se nisam čula, nekih više nema... no sve su one dio jednoga svjedočenja o vremenu u kojemu ja kao autorica nisam bitna. Vjerujem da je ovaj tekst relevantan kao jedno viđenje, kao jedno od *mogućih* viđenja. A događalo se, dapače često, da je to viđenje u stvari bio jedino što je autorici u drastičnim okolnostima o kojima je kao dijete čitala u udžbenicima i čitankama – ni ne sluteći da će ih jednom i sama proživjeti/preživjeti – bilo preostalo. U onom dakle binarnom sustavu u kojemu je „jedino bitno ima li te ili te nema", kako napisah na jednom mjestu. Osobe koje su mi bliske i koje ovdje spominjem molim da mi oproste što ih ni ne pitajući za dopuštenje nanovo uvlačim u doba iz kojega su se teškom mukom iščupale i kojega se možda ili vjerojatno ni ne žele prisjećati. Pokušala sam njihovim imenima pokazati da je individualizirana, *njihova pojedinačna* sudbina – važnija od „kolektivnih događanja" i „gibanja svijeta". S nježnošću i zahvalnošću sjećam se svih tih imena.

—Autorica
U Zadru, početkom srpnja 2004.

ACKNOWLEDGEMENTS

There is a particular aptness in the timing of this publication of this book. These days we are commemorating the eighteenth anniversary of the wanton destruction that engulfed historic Croatian cities like Vukovar and villages such as Škabrnje and Nadin. The people whose lives were destroyed in these places will remain forever engrained in our nation's memory. Those who once inhabited these towns and villages and their defenders deserve to be remembered. How many of the readers of this volume are aware of what really happened in those years? If this small volume goes some way towards witnessing to this truth and the communal dreams that were buried during those years, then it will have been a small triumph.

I would like to thank everybody who contributed to the production of this volume and made its publication in bilingual form a reality: publisher Cambridge Scholar Press for having recognized the relevance of the book, translator Petra Sapun, and proof-reader Nick Saywell, who were always generous with their knowledge and their time. In particular, I would like to thank them for their patience in seeing what was a demanding project to its conclusion.

I would also like to express my deep gratitude to a number of people who are close to my heart: my colleagues in literature, Irish writers Mícheál Ó hAodha and Gabriel Rosenstock. Their help was unflagging at all times as was that of my loyal friend and colleague Sintija Čuljat. I would also like to mention dear Ivana Haberle for providing me with some published material relating to the Homeland War.

Finally, I am grateful to all my other friends, colleagues and students in Croatia and abroad, for their good wishes, encouragement and unfailing support.

—Helena
Zadar, 18 November 2009

ZAHVALE UZ OVO IZDANJE

Postoji određena koncidencija u vremenu pisanja ove zahvale. Ovih dana bilježimo osamnaestu obljetnicu uništenja hrvatskih povijesnih gradova poput Vukovara i sela poput Škabrnje i Nadina. Ljudi koji su nekad živjeli u tim mjestima i selima te njihovi branitelji zaslužuju biti zapamćeni. Koliko je čitatelja ove knjige svjesno onoga što se doista dogodilo onih godina? Posvjedoči li ova knjižica o istini i snovima koji su bili pokopani tih godina, bit će to veliki uspjeh.

Zahvaljujem svima koji su doprinijeli objavljivanju ove knjige u dvojezičnom izdanju: prije svega, nakladniku Cambridge Scholars Publishing – što je prepoznao važnost moga teksta. Potom prevoditeljici Petri Sapun i lektoru Nicku Saywellu na njihovu znanju, vremenu te strpljenju u obavljanju zahtjevnoga posla do samoga kraja.

Želim izraziti duboku zahvalnost ljudima koji su mi bliski srcu: svojim kolegama po peru, irskim piscima Mícheálu Ó hAodhi i Gabrielu Rosenstocku. Njihova je pomoć bila nepresušna kao i pomoć moje odane prijateljice i kolegice Sintije Čuljat. Zahvaljujem dragoj Ivani Haberle na ustupanju tiskane građe o Domovinskom ratu.

Konačno, zahvaljujem svim ostalim prijateljima i kolegama te svojim studentima u Hrvatskoj i inozemstvu na dobrim željama, ohrabrenju i nepokolebljivoj potpori.

—Helena

U Zadru, 18. studenog 2009.

INTRODUCTION

"THE AESTHETICS OF WAR": SOME THOUGHTS ON HELENA PERIČIĆ'S WRITING

Until recently, the writing of war diaries or dispatches was often the preserve of men. Helena Peričić has broken the mould in this regard. She has used her pen to dig through the blood-soaked ground, the shattered detritus of war and hatred. Her diaries, her dispatches - call them what you will - relate to the tragic events that circumscribed the Homeland War, the battle for independence which the Croatian people fought in the early 1990s. Strangely, this war is one which is already forgotten in the Western European imaginary. Helena Peričić does *not* forget. As a writer she admonishes us of the moral duty we have to recall, to remember and bear testament to what has happened before, to what is happening again. Peričić's writing is about emotion. Her language and artistic sensibility are new and exciting. Her art is concerned with what happens to the human mind when it is subjected to violence and unspeakable horror. Initially, the spirit recoils from what is frightening and dangerous. It seeks shelter. But the mind is stronger than the body and it rebels in order to seek out the meaning that is at the heart of chaos. The nature that is meaning itself. The mind and the artistic sensibility that is at its core seeks to make sense of human experience, of suffering, of death, whether the body wills it or no. Helena Peričić is writing in an era when many artists and writers have retreated into themselves. They have sidled out of view. Retreated to the relative comfort of their attics and garrets. And yet we express surprise when many people today question the efficacy or utility of art, of writing. When we doubt its power to engender any form of profound philosophical change. In artistic terms Peričić's writing usurps that old tiredness; it challenges us. It is source of a fresh cultural dynamic, the dynamic of testimony and the giving of witness. Her writings asks difficult questions. It asks us to think again. What is the true and nature role of culture, art and tradition in the modern age? How can modern peoples, cultures and ethnicities better relate to one another in an era when a information seems to fly faster than the sound of the human voice? As Helena's writing demonstrates, the world may change at a bewildering pace but the nature of war, hatred and violence always remain the same. It is appropriate that her book should open with the ever-prescient words of Miroslav Krleža:

> So many have been shot that a person can easily get lost in this cemetery. Generally speaking, it is hard to tell who killed whom. Those who killed yesterday are gone today. The same as the ones that they killed, and those who will do the killing tomorrow; they too will be gone tomorrow, and those who will shoot and hang tomorrow won't have any idea that we, today, are the ones they've killed and burned at the stake. Generally speaking, it is hard to know who killed whom and why, and who is still alive and who is dead.
> —From Miroslav Krleža's *Aretej*

Like all good art, Peričić's literature is formed within the aesthetic firmament that is deep soul-searching and the fear of the unknown:

24 November 1991

On Friday, we travelled to Šibenik while the alert was in force. All the way there, I was afraid of being hit by a shell or stopped by some Serbian soldier. Between Biograd and Pakoštane, suddenly a flaming projectile flew over my head; it flashed and hissed like a shooting star. "Make a wish!" – "I wish we survive."

Or, on the following day:

25 November 1991

...what kind of violence was happening just 15 kilometres from Zadar. That distance today does not exist any more. THEY came to the edge of the city, they "beat us" day and night; they start suddenly, they cut off the electricity and water supplies, they sabotage the local radio-waves by imposing their own Radio Belgrade and Knin, they tear down – as they say – the "stones" of our churches, Romanesque rosettes, Renaissance palaces...

Peričić is not afraid to speak her mind. This is writing with a new, raw edge and with consummate skill she explores the nature of suffering, the turmoil and doubt that always lurk at the heart of the human condition:

That's where Ema and I spent last night. Even though it was officially proclaimed a shelter, that basement across the street is actually not suitable for sheltering: it is full of shelves with files from the building's offices. We removed the files, stacked them against the wall, and we slept between the shelves on boards covered with blankets. Stacked together like – files…

I've just heard that an attack on Biograd has started and that the shells are falling on the very centre of the town. The thought of death preys on my mind continuously. I pray to the angels and the saints that I do not live to see Ema's misery, that I never become a witness to the inconceivable.

Is anywhere safe? Is there any refuge left in this "fallen" world Peričić asks?:

25 December 1991

I went with Ema to visit my brother in Split for a few days. Last night, Mum and Dad ate cod with their neighbours by candlelight, in the corridor in front of the lift (which is, in a way, the "safest" place on the seventh floor of their building). Shells hit a lot of apartment buildings on Voštarnica[1].

The power of Peričić's work lies in its usurpation of the mundane, the banal aspect that is the dangerous madness of war, the very essence of modernity itself. Peričić's writing calls us back. It remonstrates with us; it demands that we remember and give testimony.

We left for Ljubljana by bus. Our bus was only one of the four or five busses that were leaving for Slovenia at the same time. There was a young woman on the bus, sitting right next to Ema and me, with an eight-day-old baby girl, lying in a newborn's crib. With a baby girl who didn't even have a name yet.

I was among the first who entered the bus so I got the chance to study the faces of the people who came aboard. Near me, an old woman was trying to sit down with the help of her friend. The old woman was very slow, so some woman behind her, about fifty years old, started pushing her and yelling. Among all those lost and teary looks of people – who were no longer capable of any kind of reaction and who just wanted to begin their journey (without ever returning?) – I was the one who had to object and cry out to the heartless, bewildered woman: "Why are you rushing this old lady? Do we really all have to be insane?"

Peričić's writing is beautiful and perceptive. It is evocative. In an age when the beauty of the world is forgotten it reminds us of the power that is

---

[1] A district in the north-east of Zadar

the written word. One can only do true justice to her work by reading it, by savouring the sensations and the memories, the words on the page. Peričić's writing is memory and poetry as one essence. As with the poetry of mystics such as Jabes and Lévinas, it is life at the living breathing edges of perception, the desert that is the human soul:

> Thought in infinite regress, writing of the abyss. At the edge. But if the trace is in me, beats within me? Every impulse of my body is a recorded, counted trace, multiplied by fever – by love, pain, delirium. The trace is tied to being, to essence, as to the emptiness with which it perhaps resonates.[2]

—Mícheál Ó hAodha *(Irish writer)*
Limerick, Ireland
January, 2010

[2] Edmond Jabes (with Emmanuel Lévinas), "There is No Trace But in the Desert", in *The Book of Margins*, translated by Rosemary Waldrop (Chicago: University of Chicago Press, 1993), p. 161.

18 July 1991

In the scorching, summer dust... All those deaths... *It is not possible to distance oneself from the sentimentality induced by war: when I first started writing this, neither I, nor anyone in my vicinity, was thinking – in literary terms.*

26 August 1991

It has already been a year since the first clashes with the Serbs in Croatia. The initial barricading of the main roads in Lika has in the meantime transformed into crimes that have not been seen since World War II. *Evil and fear of evil must be individualized. When drowned in multitude, war loses its meaning.* I am alone with Ema in the apartment. S. is in Šibenik. Every night before I fall asleep, I pray to the angels to protect the child that is sleeping so peacefully next to me. *Surely, no experience is so difficult and more painful to endure that worrying about the destiny of your own child in the drastic circumstances of war and violence...*

27 August 1991

The war continues. This sunny and quiet afternoon is in contrast to what is happening in the villages in the vicinity of Zadar. I listen to the radio and television news all the time. (I tried to avoid it the entire summer in order to stay calm, but now I am alone with Ema in our apartment and I want to be informed about what is going on around the city.) The radio: instructions in the event of an air raid on the city. S. is leaving for Zagreb tomorrow. I'm considering leaving with Ema somewhere. Maybe to the north, to Rijeka. Maybe to Lovran, to Aunt Ana's place? Would it be cowardice?

The water will be cut off again tomorrow. (Actually, just like any other day lately.) They're talking of digging new wells for drinking water within the city itself. And there's so much that needs to be washed. Ema needs a bath as well... This Ema has just turned a year and a half...

Maybe they will declare war and order a general mobilization. I wonder how long all of this will last? And when it finally does come to an end – because it has to end eventually – the confrontation will continue. Diplomacy and negotiations won't stop terrorism, explosions, cutting off water supplies... What is going to happen – afterwards?

31 August 1991

Today the deadline expires for withdrawing the army from Croatia. Because of this, some people are calling this Saturday "D-Day". I hope that we will live to see tomorrow, and the day after tomorrow, and the one after that...

1 September 1991

Images on the TV news: severed hands, eyes poked out, mutilated bodies of the dead. Everything I write seems trivial in comparison to the reality.

We are spending this weekend in Sukošan[1]. The crickets are chirping in the nearby cypresses and tamarisks like every summer. And like every summer, it is scorching, so I'm looking for some remaining currents of freshness within the "corridors" of the sheets. Just like every summer, the mosquitoes are buzzing and they seem ever more merciless and more resilient. The summer matrix of current life in northern Dalmatia is a setting for the atavistic, instinctive need for hope and belief in any kind of God, who will surely, sooner or later, bring us salvation!

5 September 1991

If by some chance a new Gertrude Stein were to appear today, maybe she would call my generation, the one born in the early 1960s, the "lost" generation. Today Branka, Rade, his brother Branko and I visited Snježana, whose brother committed suicide a couple of days ago (on Monday). He was 28 years old. He was an extremely talented young man, an electrical engineering graduate who recently got a job in Zadar and... He took his life with a revolver. With his father's revolver. Was it loneliness, or longing for some lost love or was his bright and sensitive mind already clouded by this hopeless everyday wartime life, and simply pushed over the edge by one final image of the cruelty surrounding us?

13 September 1991

Today is my birthday. A big one. *Happy birthday!*

Everyone I met and talked to today seemed to be completely awestruck. While I was at the Scientific Library – an oasis of quiet, peace and concentrated dedication to knowledge – my answering machine recorded the following messages: Tina called – she is back in Zagreb from her holiday (how I envy her for being there!); other calls from Zagreb included one from Ana – Ema's godmother – and from Branka B. They all want to know how we are doing: whether there is running water, food... Yes, there is for now, all of that, except for freedom of movement, optimism and laughter. I tried to reach Ana that afternoon at the

---

[1] A village on the coast, about ten kilometres south-east of Zadar.

Lexicographic Institute but without any success. The phone lines to Zagreb are overloaded. The situation in Zadar is terrible.

Today's news reported from Vukovar, and one of the murdered victims was a five-year-old child. I'm afraid, I'm so afraid: of the knives, the massacres, my own fear... They say that the guns are pointing towards Zadar and that the planes are ready for an air raid on the city – the city of stone, the wide city that is sunbathing in an Indian summer. There is so much sun in the city these days! How can even the sun be so weak when confronted with the smoke from the fires, with the ruins of the centuries-old city walls, with the blood shed on these ancient pavements...? Are these the last minutes of an apparent peace in these parts?

16 September 1991

Saturday's "celebration" of my thirtieth birthday was very short (my friends had already left at 9 pm). I invited some friends over, thinking it might be a good idea for all of us to get together – maybe even for the last time with some of them – *(...which proved to be right!)* in these circumstances. Even though some of them supported my intention to host this get-together, I knew that some were reluctant to come. I thought I would be a cheerful hostess who wouldn't let the party turn into too much bickering over the maladies of war. Over cookies and a few bottles of wine, everything seemed pretty "normal". And then suddenly a helicopter landed at the barracks some 30 metres away. Some of us stepped outside onto the balcony to watch it landing. Explosions began to sound from the Zadar hinterland. But when Marina P. started shivering after hearing the first detonation – her fear caused my own discomfort and some insecurity at first, and then my own first real fear, which completely paralyzed me. So I stopped engaging in conversation and nothing seemed funny anymore. (Not even Rade, who tried to pull off a couple of jokes as usual.) *Rade and his family still live in Zadar. Marina, Nenad and their baby girl live somewhere in Belgium. Tibo and Tanja live and work between Vienna and Slovenj Gradec. Cero is also in Slovenia. Snježana works as an architect in London. Apart from Snješka, I don't keep in touch with any of them.... All that is left from our student acoustic band "Lucida Intervalla" (gigs at KSET, Farmacija, the student halls of residence on the Sava...) is a mere audio tape recording.*

17 September 1991

Am I fully aware of everything that is going on in this part of the world? It's about 2 pm. Ema is asleep and I still don't know if she will manage to sleep through her afternoon nap, or if she'll be disturbed in her sleep by the sound of the sirens and our descent to the basement of a neighbouring building. That's where Ema and I spent last night. Even though it was officially proclaimed a shelter, that basement across the street is actually not suitable for sheltering: it is full of shelves with files from the building's offices. We removed the files, stacked them against the wall, and we slept between the shelves on boards covered with blankets. Stacked together like – files. Was that yesterday or the day before? – Right: on Monday – when S., Ema and I met, by sheer coincidence, for the first time in the shelter, a nuclear shelter no less. When I took Ema to the paediatrician at the hospital for her compulsory examination for admission to nursery school, we shared the shelter with the medical staff and their patients. *There are only two or three nuclear shelters in the whole of Zadar! During the war, people descended to improvised shelters (which weren't real shelters), into woodsheds and basements, in which – as it happens – many got killed.*

I've just heard that an attack on Biograd[2] has started and that the shells are falling on the very centre of the town. The thought of death preys on my mind continuously. I pray to the angels and the saints that I do not live to see Ema's misery, that I never become a witness to the inconceivable.

18 September 1991

My parents stayed at my apartment last night because it is supposedly safer than theirs, which is situated on the south-east side, seventh floor of a nearby building. I will probably remember last night for as long as I live. We spent it in the modestly furnished kitchen of my rented apartment, in complete darkness. The only thing alive in that gloomy and creepy ambiance was Ema (who just recently turned 19 months) and a battery-operated radio and cassette deck, on which we tried to record a few of the sentences she said.

I don't know how it came to this, but at one point, I said I wanted to leave Zadar with Ema, maybe even leave Croatia altogether. My father jumped up at these words and started yelling at me, threatening to renounce me if I ever even thought about leaving again. My reaction to him was even harsher. I started screaming that I wanted to protect my child, that it was impossible for a small child to live in these conditions: without electricity, water, medicine... I ran off into the bathroom, and my father followed me, yelling that I was a traitor, a traitor to my own family and my own country...

---

[2] A small town on the coast, about thirty kilometres south-east of Zadar.

20 September 1991

We left for Ljubljana by bus. Our bus was only one of the four or five busses that were leaving for Slovenia at the same time. There was a young woman on the bus, sitting right next to Ema and me, with an eight-day-old baby girl, lying in a newborn's crib. With a baby girl who didn't even have a name yet.

I was among the first who entered the bus so I got the chance to study the faces of the people who came aboard. Near me, an old woman was trying to sit down with the help of her friend. The old woman was very slow, so some woman behind her, about fifty years old, started pushing her and yelling. Among all those lost and teary looks of people – who were no longer capable of any kind of reaction and who just wanted to begin their journey (without ever returning?) – I was the one who had to object and cry out to the heartless, bewildered woman: "Why are you rushing this old lady? Do we really all have to be insane?"

Ema, my Ema, was sitting next to the window and waved goodbye to her grandma and grandpa, who were standing next to the bus. She can't speak yet. However, she can understand a great deal. She knows how to laugh beautifully with her six little teeth. I wondered if she was saving her speech for some better, more peaceful times. Grandma and Grandpa were smiling with tears in their eyes. Or crying with a smile on their faces. God knows if I'll ever see you again, I thought.

While we were driving down the road to Pag, I thought about the macchia shrubbery by the road and wondered whether some Serbian soldier might be hiding in it. We approached Pag Bridge. Some Croatian soldiers were standing on the rocky ground under the sun, in a concrete hut. They approached the bus in order to search it. I showed Ema how to make a letter "V" with her fingers, as in "victory". Of course, she did the Churchillian greeting quite poorly and clumsily. The soldier understood it nevertheless and smiled. Ema then sent him a "flying" kiss with her hand. I thought: a bit of joy for this nameless soldier with an uncertain future.

Somewhere near Crikvenica, our bus had to stop. Something was wrong with the engine. While waiting for another bus, we heard on the radio that Zadar was surrounded by tanks, so I concluded that, with the existing barrier of the sea, the city was surrounded, trapped. I remembered Dad and how he "welcomed" my decision to leave with Ema using some very harsh and ugly words about me being a coward, about me being afraid for myself rather than for Ema... I will probably never be able to get that image and my offended reaction out of my mind.

The other bus arrived an hour and a half later. While we waited, we talked to some workers at the gas station. They were afraid that the warships in front of Rijeka might start attacking the city. At Rijeka bus station, the young woman with the nameless baby in the crib smiled at Ema. *Later on, I found out that she named the baby – Ema.* We were stopped at the Slovenian border by their police and asked if all the passengers had arranged accommodation in Ljubljana. They say that Ljubljana is overpopulated and not accepting any new refugees. They offer us accommodation at Ilirska Bistrica. We will get food and shelter.

Humiliation and misery... All the passengers continue their voyage to Ljubljana anyway. They have friends and a temporary home there, where there is no panic and no warning sirens.

26 September 1991

After a few days in Ljubljana, staying with some friends, Ema and I flew to London via Klagenfurt.

1 October 1991

The following inscription stands in the centre of Westminster Abbey, in the brightest part of the church, the chapel of Edward the Confessor – the founder of the Abbey – one metre across from the wooden coronation chair dating from 1301:

"Please pray: for all places affected by war and violence, especially Yugoslavia, and for those who work to make and maintain peace."

2 October 1991

The war, the war is over there, in Croatia. We sit at Silvana's place in front of the teletext from morning till late in the night, reading the latest news from our homeland. Staying here feels absurd...

12 October 1991

"It's a rocky road that leads to democracy," said an unknown elderly woman with too much make-up on, sitting opposite me on the London underground.

"You look after yourself, dear. I would so love to visit Dubrovnik once again..."

29 October 1991

Dear Snježana!

It's about time I got in touch with you with a few words. Ema and I have arrived in Zagreb via Ljubljana, as planned, and have been here for over a week now. The situation in Croatia, as you probably know, is still confused and I doubt that it will change any time soon. The fighting is not abating, and even the situation around Zadar and Šibenik is pretty tight, with the possibility of new confrontations.

Here in Zagreb, we are staying in a very cold apartment, and since we only took the basics with us – we are living like real refugees. No London comfort here. Luckily, we have friends here so we get by. I was told that lectures at the Faculty of Philosophy in Zadar will probably start around November 4th, so I'm currently trying to prepare myself mentally for our return to Zadar. I would be very glad to hear from you. Best regards.

2 November 1991

That insane sound of the sirens!

I remember that during the night, when they were expecting a general alert to be sounded, Pavuša rang us up and warned us about this possibility and that it had been announced on the radio. *What Pavuša and his Department for Protection of Cultural Landmarks did during the war, "patching up" buildings the day after they were bombed – was a heroic undertaking, which is forgotten too easily!* My parents spent that night at our apartment. I called some people to share the news with them. None of us knew what it would be like, were we really going to be attacked, would there be ruins, casualties... We were scared of meeting the monster that was knocking on our door.

3 November 1991

For a few days, I was occupied with the words of *Dulce et Decorum Est* by Wilfred Owen who sarcastically alluded to the Latin idea of a sweet and honourable death for one's country. The atrocities of World War I, which were described by the English poets of his generation, seem like a child's game in comparison to what is happening today in Croatia.

Candles have been burning in Zagreb windows these past few days. Everyone was advised to stay at home, because the cemeteries were possible bombing targets and places of possible shootings in general. Still, many people went to the cemeteries both for All Hallows Eve and All Saints' Day. It was a much more courageous thing to do in Slavonia, Dalmatia...

Ema is still coughing, her nose is still running, and her cold is not getting any better. It's so cold here in Zagreb! We get up late, after nine, in order to avoid the cold; and even at that hour – as we hear on the radio news – the temperature is around zero. Yesterday the sirens announced a general alert at about 4 pm, and today at about 3 pm. In both cases, at S.'s suggestion (or order?), we didn't hide anywhere; we stayed in the apartment, which was on the top floor, under a flat roof.

The public was concerned mostly by what was going on in Dubrovnik, so yesterday's attack on Zadar was barely even mentioned on the TV news. Every time I hear the sirens, I see images of children with bodies mutilated by bombs, of children in hospitals, children with big, scared eyes who don't understand a thing, who can't even ask why. I see helpless newborns born in hospital basements, right next to adult patients, psychiatric patients, trauma patients... A few days ago, a girl named Neža was born in the shelter of Vukovar hospital (or of what is left of it). *A baby girl was born!* Could that first cry of a baby, of a new life, make Neža's mother happy? How is it to create life that is screaming and crying at its first breath of the stale basement air, that is screaming to express the horror and humiliation of a tiny person created just so it can put his or her piece into the mosaic of the turmoil of high politics and ideology? What are those devices, those flesh-grinding machines that sacrifice everything? Even life before life.

A journalist from Vukovar warns that his city has been forgotten by the Croatian public and Croatian politicians. (Isn't it the same with Zadar?) People are dying in Vukovar while elsewhere (unsuccessful) negotiations are taking place.

I often think of Snježana's brother who chose for himself the time and the way he would end his life. I wonder if he had predicted everything that was going to happen, and everything that is now happening in Zadar. I must have made things harder for Snježana with my visit and my sinister tales of going to the shelters. I've noticed that she's adopted some very British characteristics: composure and keeping aloof. She is probably aware of the necessity of being like that, fighting for her job and survival in the context of today's recession- and inflation-ridden Britain with almost three million unemployed.

4 November 1991

Albert Primorac... On the radio news a plea for the girlfriend of Albert Primorac, wounded in Banija, to get in touch with his mother. Albert Primorac... How many other Alberts have already been wounded or killed? For how many Alberts will a candle be burning these days and every other All Saints' Day from now on?

5 November 1991

Ema and I left Zagreb and went to Zadar. The lectures at the faculty start tomorrow. They've enforced compulsory working. I wonder how a one-and-a-half-year-old will manage in these conditions.

7 November 1991

It's Mum and Dad's anniversary today: their 32nd in a row. They've earned a much more cheerful anniversary.

(I haven't had my period for the past two months. And I'm definitely not pregnant, unless I was paid a visit by the Holy Spirit. There's obviously something wrong with my metabolism. Or is it a stress-related disorder?)

19 November 1991

It's started again. They've started again...

Since yesterday at 9:30 am, both an air-raid alert and the so-called general alert have been in force in Zadar. People should be in shelters. First attacks on Nadin and Škabrnja began, then they continued with artillery and air attacks on Zadar. They took about 80 women, children and old people from Škabrnja to Benkovac yesterday; three were killed on the spot. *In Sukošan cemetery: six graves, one next to the other, in black marble; graves of young men butchered in Škabrnja, with whom my brother used to play basketball...* This morning, we found out that several people in Zadar were killed as well, and several people shot; St Anastasia's Church and St Chrysogonus' were hit, as well as many other churches and buildings in Zadar. What awaits us – only God knows. *The Sukošan basketball team is not doing so well today: there are no generations between the cadets and seniors.*

21 November 1991

Fourth anniversary of a (failed) marriage.

24 November 1991

On Friday, we travelled to Šibenik while the alert was in force. All the way there, I was afraid of being hit by a shell or stopped by some Serbian soldier. Between Biograd and Pakoštane, suddenly a flaming projectile flew over my head; it flashed and hissed like a shooting star. "Make a wish!" – "I wish we survive."

It's relatively peaceful in Šibenik. The fighting is going on behind Skradin so the alerts are usually heard in the villages on the north-western coastline. We are staying at S.'s parents on the 2nd floor, under the roof without a "slab", but in a case of an alert, we can go down into the garage, which is partly buried in the ground. I should go to Zadar tomorrow, to work. Ema will probably stay here. I think it's peaceful in Zadar now and there's no alert in force. However, there's still no electricity or water. We should vaccinate Ema here, because it can't be done in Zadar since there's no electricity.

You and I in two
city-winners
defeated winners[3]

25 November 1991

Dear Professor Vidan![4]

On Friday morning, while the alert was in force, I drove my family to Šibenik to stay with my husband's parents. Even if I wanted to, I could not possibly tell you what it has been like in Zadar for the past few days. Suffice to say, on our way to Šibenik, somewhere around Biograd, shells flew over our heads.

On Saturday, during a phone call with my parents, I learned that your letter with a copy of the offprint from the Belgrade meeting has arrived. I had "given up" on publishing those seminars a long time ago – but still we managed to get them, via Sarajevo. My father read part of your letter to me over the phone, and it both moved and delighted me. Thank you very much for that. Regarding the lectures at our faculty, they have been postponed "until further notice".

I haven't spent the entire war period in Zadar. The same day the barricades were raised in Zadar, I travelled to Ljubljana with little Ema. Then I travelled to my cousin's in London, where Ema and I spent three weeks.

I know that my leaving for England – while my home town was being bombed, its citizens killed and children like my own living in shelters – might be considered an act of treason. However, above all, I wanted to protect Ema from the violence, from its images and sounds. (Ema usually reacts to each explosion by pointing her finger in the direction where the sound of the explosion came from and saying her moving onomatopoeia "dum-dum".)

I don't know if you remember when I mentioned in my letter last spring what kind of violence was happening just 15 kilometres from Zadar. That distance today does not exist any more. THEY came to the edge of the city, they "beat us" day and night; they start suddenly, they cut off the electricity and water supplies, they sabotage the local radio-waves by imposing their own Radio Belgrade and Knin, they tear down – as they say – the "stones" of our churches, Romanesque rosettes, Renaissance

---

[3] From my lyrical fragment *A Tale of Two Cities*.

[4] Professor Ivo Vidan was the renowned Anglicist who passed away in 2003.

palaces, Baroque concert halls... *In June 1999, the restoration of the last unrestored cultural landmark in our town – the Duke's Palace – was finally began ...*; our vineyards and olive groves are turned into mine fields, and they play a game of "hide-and-seek" on our bridges... They massacre and hang, making real physical and psychological cripples out of the children. How many traumatized generations? How many deaths, Professor? How many lost loves, lost gentleness, parental care, how many desperate children's looks, and finally: how many encouragements for compassion from which – as the Greatest writes in *Lear* – "you can wither away".

All the best.

Your former student,

Helena Peričić

27 November 1991

Dear Jasenka,

I am not sure if I'll be able to send this letter to you. It seems as if I've written it hundreds of times in my head, and now I don't know how to put it all down on paper.

What is happening to us here cannot simply be called horror (or maybe the word "horror" has just lost its weight along the way?). Šibenik is currently peaceful, but as you yourself are well aware, peace can turn into hell and destruction very easily. In any case, the situation is such that one cannot do anything sensible, or create anything, but one can think a lot about all of it, and go mad, slowly. Next to my bed is an alarm clock. The radio is silent and the clock display shows no sign of numbers, just fluorescent red lines and a blinking little dot. Time stands still. Ema is asleep next to me. There are some newspaper cuttings on the destruction of Zadar on my bedside table, among them the one written by Pavuša and published in *Dalmacija* last Thursday. I'm a bit fed up with Šibenik. I don't do any work here because I didn't get the chance to bring my books along with me. I'm rereading *King Lear*. It feels absurd to deal with Krišković (my potential PhD thesis) these days. Everything is absurd...

The war has turned S. into a mummy who spends day and night reading newspapers: *Dalmacija – Nedjeljna* and *Slobodna, Danas, Newsweek*, stupid things, idiocies (I quote Aralica on this one).

I long for gentleness, attention. I get no hugs, let alone kisses. And something "stronger" is out of the question. Last night, I suggested having sex to S. for the first time in a month. He didn't even lift his eyes from his newspaper. He mumbled almost with disgust: "Hm?"

Love,

Helena

28 November 1991

I was angry with S. today when he refused to kiss me in the kitchen, after lunch. Apart from us, his grandmother was the only person in the kitchen, but she was doing the dishes at that particular moment and had her back turned to us. I left the kitchen abruptly and slammed the door in anger. I don't think he understands a thing. That is just what I said to him: "I think I may even understand you, whereas you don't even try to understand me."

I know there's a war going on, that people are dying, that children are being slaughtered. I know that S. is terrified by the idea of being drafted. But: do I really have to think about these things all the time? Don't I have rights, like everyone else, to allow myself even for just a moment to forget all the atrocities and just for a brief second momentarily, seemingly shut myself out of everything? Besides, I need something to give me a bit of strength for all that lies ahead of us.

In order to calm down the tension between us, S. took me to the bathroom in the evening where we allowed ourselves the luxury of a kissing session for two minutes.

25 December 1991

I went with Ema to visit my brother in Split for a few days. Last night, Mum and Dad ate cod with their neighbours by candlelight, in the corridor in front of the lift (which is, in a way, the "safest" place on the seventh floor of their building). Shells hit a lot of apartment buildings on Voštarnica[5].

30 December 1991

—in the ruined hall
among the reliquaries of glitter and velvet
a black piano
on which we used to
with children's fingers
spill (never understanding) Chopin's patriotism
Croatian polonaises are played elsewhere—[6]

25 February 1992

S. has gone off to sea. He left us in the company of bombs.

---

[5] A district in north-east Zadar
[6] A fragment from my lyrical note

19 May 1992

Our neighbours' clock has just struck eight o'clock. I light a candle for the nth time. A minute ago, I phoned Jasenka for the nth time. I'm boring her with my phone calls. It was pretty bad in Zadar yesterday. Six people were killed, among them a little girl. In M. Orešković Street. I was told about it by Professor Nevenka Brozović. For the hundredth time, Ema and I sing *Moja Domovina*[7] and I wonder: How many more times? How many more meaningless times?

26 May 1992

Dusk. Beethoven is playing from an apartment in the building opposite. The mysterious sound of the piano is intertwined with explosions from Dračevac[8]. Or maybe Bibinje[9]. *I remember even today the medlar tree under my landlord's balcony and that night with all those bright stars. I can smell the leaves and its fruits. I really can. How many times in the meantime, since that very night have I felt, do I feel something? How much love and hate was expected from me in the meantime?*

News from Sarajevo. Arkan is dead? Really? Assassination attempt on Šešelj. Unsuccessful. They are bombing the Sarajevo maternity hospital that is sheltering mothers and 170 children in its basement. I wonder: where does this human bestiality end? How much hate does one need to possess in order to slaughter a woman with a baby in her womb?

29 May 1992

Tonight I dine alone at the table, with a candle and a petroleum lamp. And I stare at Snježana's scented London letter. My hands are sticky and I want to remove this uncomfortable feeling with sleep. But sleep won't come.

A cigarette? No: I get nauseous. Music on the radio – bad. I'll wait for the news. The petroleum lamp is hissing. The shadows it casts on the wall are silhouettes of my lost (forgotten?) loves. Oh God, I want to live a different life! I'm trying to make a candle out of the leftovers of several old ones. What an idiotic undertaking. A damp, before-the-rain evening. Swarms of flies in the kitchen. I think about those damp, greyish mornings in London, with the sky hanging over the city, and the scents of tea and spices brewing from cheap Italian and Indian stores...

---

[7] "My Homeland", a very popular Croatian patriotic song during the war

[8] A village near Zadar

[9] A village some four kilometres from Zadar, situated on the coast

30 May 1992

THE RED HORSE AND THE THREE IVANS
(three stories of violence)

A rider on his red horse, with a sword in his hand, rides at full gallop.

Radio: *witnesses – victims – executors...* I wonder if there is a measure for hate, a systematicness of violence, counterpart to evil. Even that landlord from Jasna Poljana, who tried to figure out the laws of war and peace, wrote long ago how he would like to actually live his life, not merely *guard over it*.

A branch of myrtle in a simple glass vase flabbergasts me with its indifference.

* * *

Story I
May 1967
Zadar, Vladimir Nazor Park

They beat him up. The two of them. I remember it well. One of them actually just held him under his armpits so that the other one could hit him with more precision in the face and stomach. With his fists. There were no voices. Just blunt hits and grunts.

Our "nanny" instantly stopped talking with the kindergarten teacher of the other group, turned to us and said:

"Look there, children, at that tree with the light yellow flowers. That's myrtle. Myrtle smells wonderful."

I don't know if the others looked at the myrtle. I doubt it. I sure didn't. However, it managed to impose itself on me with its heavy, too heavy smell. The dark green vegetation and the coolness of the park looked tame and protective a moment ago. Now they seemed like a dark and stuffy place one needed to get away from.

We walked in a line, two by two. Without making a sound. Most of us with our heads down. I noticed that the two attackers suddenly disappeared, leaving their victim on the ground. As we got closer, he tried to stand up. He staggered and tottered. Finally, he leaned on a tree and pressed his hand on his stomach, vomiting. The stuff running out of his mouth to the ground reminded me, at the time, of those dark red nylon threads that my uncle used as fishing line.

Ivan walked beside me. We held hands as kindergarten kids usually do. He noticed how I watched the bent-over boy the entire time and squeezed my hand reprovingly.

"You're stupid!" Ivan said and pointed with his finger to our nanny.

The smell of myrtle gradually started reflecting inside me as an unstoppable tide wave of disgust and nausea.

At one point, I began thinking how Ivan knew nothing.

He really KNEW NOTHING.

Story II

November 1991

Village near Zadar

Father stormed into the house. He told Mum to take Kata. We heard shots and the sound of an engine. It was a truck. I know that for sure. Katarina started crying. She's still little. I'm big.

Dad took some kind of an envelope out of the shoe cabinet. And a knife. He took a black plastic garbage bag and stuffed some clothes into it. He didn't mind my watching him. When Dad is in hurry, he doesn't like me milling around. That's what he says.

Then he grabbed my hand. We all ran out into the courtyard. From there, we could hear Aunt Rose yelling: "People, help me! Help me!" Then suddenly screams. Then grunts.

Mum and Dad ran to the fields with Kata in their arms. I watched them disappear. Then dad turned around and yelled:

"Ivan, son, are you mad? Why aren't you running?"

"I can't, Dad", I said. "I can't move."

Dad hugged me. He had big eyes. Then he took me into his arms and ran after Mum and Kata. He carried me and the black plastic bag; the envelope and the knife in his pocket. As Dad was losing his breath, he whispered:

"YOU KNOW NOTHING, my Ivan. And thank God you don't..."

Story III

May 1992

Zadar, Voštarnica district

"Hit him, Maja, hit him! Goddamnit. You don't know a thing! Eh... You shouldn't show him any mercy."

They hit him with a plastic tube that had water running through it, they beat him, stretched his limbs, squirted water into his eyes, stuffed his head into garbage bags, finally bringing him to the open doors of the woodshed, placing his head between the door and doorpost, and tried to jam it, crush it.

He squealed, howled. He stood over the flooded yard with his legs stretched. Like Moses in front of the Red Sea. Waiting for a miracle to save him.

The girl screamed in the trance of the torture ritual. Like some voodoo priestess. Ivan encouraged her and scolded her for being too merciful. He was the boss of the courtyard. Maybe even of the entire block. He had a dog and knew how to handle him. He knew everything.

This Ivan KNEW EVERYTHING.

* * *

Perpetuum mobile of (non)recognition of evil. Around ten o'clock. In candlelight. Explosions in the distance. Under the roofs. Under the eyelids. Inside the brain.

Latest news: *witnesses – victims – executors...*

The rider on his red horse rides at full gallop.

The branch of myrtle remains eerily indifferent.

22 July 1992

I submitted my request for a divorce. *My daughter Ema hasn't seen her father in years. I don't know what happens to people. I don't know what happened to me.*

5 September 1992

"What is the matter, my lord?"

"Between who?"

I remember how my grandmother Marija, born in Mravinci in the Split hinterland, near the end of her life, astounded and terrified by the evil that was spreading more and more, how my grandma, my Mravinka[10], who never learned how to pronounce the word "yoghurt" properly so she always said "yorguth" – how she used to say that the EN' OF THE WORLD was near.

And this grandma of mine, my Mravinka, who wore a headscarf all her life – in her old age, a black head scarf covered her hair whiter than snow – this grandma of mine used to say that the EN' OF THE WORLD was approaching.

This grandma of mine, who spent the last years of her life on the hated seventh floor of some concrete monster – because there was no one left in

[10] Term for a woman originating from the village of Mravinci (near Split)

the countryside to take care of her (or be taken care of), this grandma of mine used to say that the EN' OF THE WORLD was near.

This grandma of mine, who used to braid my hair soaking it in spit when I was a little girl (because that's how she braided her own hair when she was a young girl during World War I) – and which disgusted me somewhat – this grandma of mine, wiser than Solomon, she used to say that the EN' OF THE WORLD was approaching.

God provided (as she used to say), and my favourite Mravinka did not live long enough to even get a glimpse of all the things she predicted so disappointedly.

* * *

Physical, superficial, bloody violence which cannot be grasped and taken in by a human mind (however composed) without resulting in disgust and abhorrence as the only possible defence (in order to stay sane and not feel completely powerless) – such violence is not the only kind welcoming us with open arms in these times. Violence may be lurking in some far less obvious places: in the pores and molecules of human existence, which are not so obvious and tangible.

One needs to remember all those miserable treasures we used to carry in our purses or plastic bags into the woodsheds, basements and shelters, or which we – when deciding to stay in our apartments during the alert – held by our side as something that needs to be close at hand because it contains the essence of ourselves and of life itself?

All those documents with signatures and stamps, some jewellery and a few letters, photos of fieldtrips, all our tectonic passions and longings in life, masked by seeming indifference... But has the war taught us to appreciate this same life more than we used to before?

All those hugs that we gave each other at the end of every alert, warmly and almost mad with joy after exiting into the light, the sun and daily routines – they gradually turned into its Mephistophelean dark side: poverty, envy, bitterness, cynicism, revengefulness, lust for power... Hiding our own mistakes and sins from ourselves, we become "Christians" who cross themselves energetically and call out His name too often, carrying only one real belief within: that God created his own image first. I remember the obituaries whose pathos lasted as long as the daily papers – just for a day; I remember students wearing black clothes – mourning their fellow students; children who need (despite everything!) to be retaught children's games... However, this rolling stone of *our* daily lives will hit the wall of getting upset idiotically and unnecessarily because of God knows what; that blasé attitude towards other people's misery turned into carelessly overheard gossip; people's unhappiness at their worth being trivialized as a mere label: pro/anti-Serb, pro/anti-Communist, pro/anti-Yugoslav, pro/anti-homosexuality, promiscuity, prostitution... And all of which will finally be towered over by powerful, relentless and utterly overpowering dissection, tormenting, accusations and judgments in (too) long newspaper articles. Invisible, paper enemies, so "courageous", will throw the gauntlet into each others faces instead of a rock (masking their verbal violence behind a veneer of fine manners!) to finally become themselves the real victims, after the duel is over, victims whose paper articles will be read – by seconds *passa tempo* (allegedly) of hurt vanity, seconds of the intimate and true EN' OF THE WORLD.

"I mean, the matter that you read, my lord."

"*S l a n d e r s, sir...*"[11]

13 September 1992

I think about Budapest.

I think about the lights that spread across the huge bridges over the Danube. I was drinking a *caffè latte* at a small restaurant on a wide street in the city centre. Their restaurants did not seem as ready-made and luxurious as most restaurants in Zagreb and small cafes on the coast. Budapest! It lay before us like some half-naked dancer painted by Toulouse-Lautrec (wasn't "dancer" an unnecessary Secession euphemism for "courtesan"?). Nevertheless, Budapest was trully lushious with its cluttered shopping windows – ear lobes mercilessly weighted with cheap and heavy earrings; with curtains on windows – wrinkled lace on its swollen breasts; with fluorescent posters that tried to unsuccessfully mimic the plenty of Western Europe, but reached only as far as its suburbs with a theme park decorated by colourful lights. Ah, Budapest! We could smell the fresh pastries near us (the kind that are only made in Budapest: with walnuts, blueberry jam or with chocolate fudge...). He wanted me to have a good time there. He tried so hard: a young lover who was scared of making a mistake at every single moment. He was confused and distracted, and he rarely managed to pull something off in the way he intended to. But that's exactly what was so sweet about him, and why he was so impressionable. Almost to tears.

I was scared of being spoiled and whimsical, of my power to ask for whatever I wanted, the supremacy that can easily cover up the fact that this same girl was entering what we refer to as – the dangerous age.

[11] The quotes are from *Hamlet,* naturally.

3 October 1992
Divorce.

1 November 1992
Tonight, one of Zadar's most promising actors – a puppeteer – Srećko Šestan left Zadar. He left me his "pony bicycle", not knowing what to do with it. He, by leaving the town, and I, by accepting the bicycle, have by mere accident entered the newly established ranks of war profiteers.

13 November 1992
Stain
A wine stain on the yellow tablecloth.
I say red, you assert black.
You assert black, I say red.
Black as: "nebulous", "I didn't know", "tension"...
Red as: "I need you", "I'm suffering", "mistress"...

Black and red blended into a stain.
You assert black, I say red.
Red and black spilt over the horizontal line of souls and indifference.
Black as: "I'll call you", "I'm busy", "you're overreacting"...
Red as: "call me", "I adore you", "to hell with it"...[12]

25 November 1992

CARPE DIEM
(A Story of He and She)

She wants to tell him everything. There is no time. He's leaving. He. *At midnight.* [13]
"I..."
He covers her mouth with his hand. She saw his lower teeth. They were yellow from nicotine. They were the most beautiful teeth she had ever seen. She thought how she was being hysteric.
He shut her mouth with a kiss.
D. H. Lawrence. Frenzy. *Carpe diem.* Seize the day. *No: seize the second. A fraction of a second!*

[12] My poem from the early nineties
[13] The italics in this story are an inseparable element of the discourse.

“Are you mad at me?” She asked while helping him /carry his travelling bag. At five to twelve. The pavement on Kalelarga[14] was slippery. Five to twelve.
“No,” He said. *Or perhaps he just shook his head.* She no longer remembers.

Actually, she was happy. Just a phrase? *No. Maybe more than ever. Ever* ***before****. God, that's already ... Past tense. Than ever. At least in the past thirty years.* He doesn't believe her. How could he? And she could have. And it happened. She dared to. Sparks happened.

“I'll call you.”
“I hope so.”
“I said I will.”
Gallant men. Courteous. Kind. Approbation. I hope not.
“But you could write to me...”
What? Sentimental letters, pathetic vomit. Dilettantish fiction. Tatiana writing to Onegin. And she knew how that ended. She was dumped. Spasiba. Djevuška.[15] *Djevojčura.*[16] *Without pride or dignity. So unconventional. Head through wall. Without shame.*

“Don't worry. I will visit.”
“I'm not worried, I'm just processing all of what has happened to me. What has happened to US.”
He kissed her.
“You're so wonderfully sentimental,” He said and turned his back.

Who do you think you are! Mephistopheles wanted to yell, *I started to adore, bare to the bone, and you threw that adoration like a crumb from the table... Take it or leave it.*

“Why did you run away? Wait!”
He drank back some kind of red drink. He started talking about himself, about the people around them... She was offended by their offending him. She heard every fifth word. She understood every tenth.

---

[14] The main street in the centre of Zadar
[15] Russian expression for a young girl
[16] Croatian expression for a hussy

She was drunk. With him. With happiness. *Ah, triviality. About the term: trivial literature – P. Pavličić or M. Solar*[17]*? Who knows? Luck is a trivial thing.*
She spoke nonsense. She was sentimental. Her hands quivered.
She was breathing heavily, without a word, **incapable** of saying anything. Finally she said:
"Why are you telling me this? Why all the excuses? You know I admire you!"
He looked into her eyes. She thought she was sinking. *Precioza.*
"Give me your hand," She said.
Hand in hand. Fingers intertwined.
Her hands slowly let go of the embrace. He traces her movement with a look.

She found HIM. He starts his journey in one hour. Maybe a bit later. *Ah: later. That's a real fortune. That one hour. But it doesn't matter. That he goes on a journey.*
She looks at him. Touches his cheek with her fingers. He takes her hand and presses it against his lips.
She breathed heavily.

"I'm afraid that in the morning everything will seem like a dream," She told him.
"Well this is a dream," He said.

Just a dream.
They found a caterpillar inside an Egyptian tomb. The insect turned into a butterfly after being exposed to fresh air for the first time in thousands of years. A huge, colourful, pearly-purple-turquoise. The butterfly came to life. It lived for an hour. Maybe a bit more. Well that is a real fortune. Then it dies. Burnt. In a moment.

Who do you think you are! Mephistopheles wanted to yell, *I started to adore, bare to the bone, and you threw that adoration like a crumb from the table... Take it or leave it.*

"I'm very busy," came the words out of the telephone receiver.
"Can you hear me?" He asks after a short break.
"Yes, I'm here."
She didn't know anything about him. *I adore him.*

[17] Croatian literary theorists

She breathed heavily.
"No, no I can't tell you. It's a delicate matter. Don't get mad. I'll tell you when I see you. When I arrive..."
The seagulls were slamming their wings into the window of the room on the top floor. *Silly birds.*
Humming of the computer. Twinkling lights on the islands.
Today, it seems as if someone covered the sun with a black cloth. *Suddenly. Out of spite. Ill will. When are we finally going to start acting like Dalmatians?*

She was stark naked in front of him. He didn't trust her. Her. That woman. *Frustrated woman. Suspicious woman.* And her interests? *Interests!? Good God.*

An encore after a finished show? Acting, She thought and clenched her teeth.
But I am not a theatre person, and I don't give tuppence for Brecht's theory; I cannot distance myself from this, I am EXPERIENCING it, this very moment, till the end, me, me, me, this is me, maaaaan! Obsessed with myself. Obsessed with you. This doesn't happen to me every fifteen days. Or every month. Like menstruation. Like some psychosomatic disorder.
"I'm twinkling. Ah, I need you." *(So banal, so true.)*

"Give me will, strength, that's all I ask," She said. "You want to conquer the world? O.K. I'll help you conquer it. Give me strength and I'll conquer my own. This little one. It's not much. But it's mine. Give me strength and I'll give it to you. Do you hear me? DO YOU HEAR MEEEEE? Naturally, you think all this is crazy."
Folie.

"I'm busy," the words came out of the telephone receiver, "So I can't act like some drunken..."
The sentence wasn't finished. *Those phones...*

Don't let me say the things that are trying to burst from my breast. They want to scream into the night. To slam their wings into the window on the top floor. Like a seagull. To disperse among the twinkling island lights. Like a dream.
Calvary. Hope. Restaurant Roko. And his brothers.[18] Passion. Strength. Sex. SEXplicit. Dark. Ooooh-yes to sex. Hot and heavy. *P. B. Shelley.*[19]

---

[18] Allusion to *Rocco e i suoi fratelli* (English: *Rocco and His Brothers)*, a 1960

Good God. I'm dying.
"You're so wonderfully sentimental," He said and turned his back.

Like a dream.
SOMETHING SPARKLED. A butterfly. Pearl-purple-turquoise. Burnt. In a moment. *Carpe diem.*

28 November 1992
(at the meeting of my Department at the Faculty of Philosophy)[20]

Me: I wanted to add to what Prof. D. Purely said about "correct interpersonal relations". I would therefore ask certain persons – who denied me access to the books from the Institute's library and told me to go look for them elsewhere, "considering my behaviour" – not to do that again.

Lady Macbeth: Colleague Petričić...

Me: Peričić, Madam, Peričić... At first I wished someone would explain. But I quickly realized that there was a vote going on. Not only was I offended but genuinely shocked. And all this because of my abstention during a debate about the behaviour of some colleagues who noticed some irregularities during exams; just because I expressed my support for them and abstained from voting...

Sandman (acting surprised): But you have the absolute right to abstain...

Me: Colleague Sandman, I repeat – because of my abstention...

Lady Macbeth (to herself): You think you are the most brilliant person in this Department... (She told a colleague from Macedonia that she was behaving "Balkanically", that she should return to Macedonia and learn that in Zadar, one should behave properly /??!!/. I, by contrast, got off heavenly: "Sophisticated"!)

Lady Macbeth: But I said...

Me (raised voice, ready to burst): Please, Madam librarian...

Lady Macbeth: I typed the approval for your employment...

Me: I respect that and I'm grateful to you...

Italian and French film directed by Luchino Visconti.

[19] The word "ševa" in Croatian both means a skylark and, colloquially, "a screw", i.e. sex, hence the association between sex and Shelley in the author's mind (N. S.)

[20] Even today not much has changed at the location described in 1992. People in academic positions seem to have too much free intellectual time and unconstructive energy, which are often used on constructions, scheming and imputations. "Croatian envy" was conceived, I firmly believe, in academic circles. Despite their so called humanist distinctiveness.

Columbo: ... And I graded and signed it...

Me: Well, Professor, you must have had some reason for that!!!

After the "fiesta", on the corridor, Dr. Fox winked at me and the Funny-Curly blew me a kiss.

(Dr. Fox: Since that mutiny in 1992, nothing in the Department has been fixed.)

4 December 1992

Hi.[21]

I'm becoming an egocentric. I always was one, as it turns out. (For the type of jobs that the two of us do, one probably requires a certain amount of self-righteousness.) In this town, a person lives like some kind of primitive organism, which feeds on itself. It feasts on its own cells, its own flesh. Until it is used up. Since the first moment, I offered you my trust, even though I know I still haven't got yours (nor ever will?). All that suspicion – so typical of women (but men as well) who in these situations tend to calculate and manoeuvre, understanding seduction (will you or won't you: that's all there is to it!) as some kind of diplomatic negotiation – gets on my nerves. I think it's just silly affectation. I don't know how to behave like that. I wasn't raised "well". You can trust me but you don't have to. Everything I told you about myself – is true. *Maybe it's those same people who don't own the necessary (or superfluous?) mechanisms of distancing themselves who are the ones who cause doubt. Besides, there are people who think Medea was just a crazy, hysteric old woman, and Emma Bovary a harlot, aren't there? I don't know if you understand me, but I hope – if it turns out that you despise all of this – that I won't experience the same destiny as in that story, that everyone will say: "The Emperor has no clothes!"*

I heard you're on a trip. I'm sorry, but I need to hear from you from time to time. It was especially important for me to hear from you this particular week.

I'm trying to work as much as possible. Lately, I'd really like to work on something of "mine", but I'm not allowed to. I have to do what I have to do. It consumes so much of my energy. It affects (as I am aware) my relationship with Ema and others. It's simply my obligation, my Sisyphean stone, and my PhD thesis is incredibly demanding. I sometimes stay at the faculty until 6 pm. I used to borrow the faculty computer and work from home at weekends, but now I come to the faculty on Saturdays. I wish I could stay here at night as well (I need to occupy myself with something), but I can't neglect Ema.

---

[21] A letter I never sent.

She is divine. When I say this, I think of her as of a child in general, not just **my own** *child. At night, when she sleeps, I watch her, so peaceful, with her eyes closed and breathing evenly, and then I think with great respect how in that silence and sleep in those fragile children's bodies – lies immeasurable dignity and supremacy. (Like a sphinx that guards the solution to a fatal riddle.)*

Good night. Sleep tight. Take care.

(I am not the person you take me for – he said...)

28 December 1992

I feel
as if someone has turned my soul inside out
like the pockets of a coat,
and is cutting them open with scissors
so nothing can fit in them any more.
Happy New Year!

29 December 1992

What do you think, what would I give to see once again that look you gave me in the theatre foyer, which lasted for maybe six or seven seconds? *Looks... Jorganović*[22]... If only this wasn't just a part of a game whose rules I don't know!

30 December 1992

I've become a *persona non grata*. Maybe you should avoid me. And don't call me so "often" on the phone: it might *cost* you a lot.

Maybe even a coin a week. Five heartbeats.

31 December 1992

I tried to get drunk on Sunday evening. (And I don't usually drink.) However, I only half managed to do so. That was my first attempt in my whole life. Žlahtina[23] from Vrbnik. At the restaurant Basket... I'm starting to gradually pick up the café manners of Zadar intellectuals...

God knows what will become of me in a couple of months. Maybe it would be best if I were hit by a car.

---

[22] Rikard Jorgovanić, Croatian author (1853-1880)

[23] White wine

20 February 1993

The eightieth birthday of the maestro of our literature, the number one living Croatian author – Ranko Marinković: "War. War is something much more terrifying than all of its symbols..."[24]

15 March 1993

I received a letter from the Vatican, from Monsignor C. Sepe, on behalf of Pope John Paul II, as an answer to my appeal to the Pope to protect Croatia. *Do you know how many people have profited since that day to today from their "patriotism"? Some of them are members of the "200 richest Croatian families", aren't they?*

18 March 1993 (Radio show *Despite – Usprkos*)

INTRODUCTION: Two weeks have passed since the last *Despite*. There was the Bora[25], there was the south wind and sometimes "Orkan"[26] (hurricane) as well. However, despite these weather and other conditions, we have prepared a new episode for you...

"Boris (*Boris remains to this day one of the funniest and certainly most pleasant voices on air in Zadar*), do you know the difference between Lassie and a Dalmatian[27]?"

"I have no idea. What is it?"

"Lassie comes home and a Dalmatian never does."

25 March 1993

Dear Pavle[28],

To tell you the truth, I don't really know where to begin. As you can see, I'm writing to you on a computer. My own, man, mine. A Macintosh Classic. It works as long as there is electricity in Zadar. Which is not so often.

I hope you are recovering well too. I was at the presentation of your book. I suppose Edi and Šenol have already handed their "report" on that to you.

---

[24] Marinković's words. Ranko Marinković, Croatian writer (1913-2001)

[25] A strong, cold, dry north-east wind blowing in the upper Adriatic

[26] "Orkan" was the name of a military operation of the Croatian army in the Homeland War. "Orkan" means "hurricane".

[27] Both a term for a dog breed and a native of Dalmatia.

[28] Pavle is the Croatian form of the English name Paul. The letter was written to Pavle who was at that time receiving medical treatment in the US as a Homeland War veteran.

Allow me to humbly tell you something about myself: a lot has happened (or maybe not so much) to me in the last six months. At the beginning of October, I managed to get a divorce. I won't go into details because it's something we both share the blame for. I simply made the first move because I couldn't go on like that. I'm alone now. It's pretty hard for me to be alone in this war because sometimes I wish someone would just put their hand round my shoulder and say: Everything is going to be O.K. (Even if it was a joke.) Also, pretending to be cheerful (or rather act as a monkey!) for Ema, while bombs are falling around us in a 30-metre radius is not the easiest thing in the world.

Lately I've been trying to do something for this city. I started editing and moderating a show called *Despite* on Donat FM (about culture, literature, student life – basically all those things that Zadar – doesn't have). **Despite** everything. I write almost all the contributions myself. You know, you could write something and send it to me. Really, get back to me on that. Write about whatever you want. And while you write, think about me reading that same text at around 10 pm, sitting with my back to a (open) window, half a metre away, the only thing separating me from the north-east. And you know what comes to us from that direction. The vampires start to wake up exactly around 10 pm.

Also, I've been trying to start a literary journal with some of my colleagues (and students). The whole project is still in its infancy (in "Pampers", as they say today) so it might be best not to mention it at all. You know all too well how every initiative in Zadar ends: they are cut to the ground. Those who actually could do something, keep on sitting in their armchairs saying to themselves how "something should be done". With the conflicts between the City and the County – no one knows whose city this is.

I've been trying to do something with my life (which has been pretty miserable lately). I think I might – if nothing happens to motivate me soon – go to hell. I will collapse, honestly. In every possible way. This city is killing me, man. In the past two days, I've heard about five people leaving town. Some left for New Zealand. And this is the "uplifting" news for me, can you imagine? I'm drowning gradually in this swamp of silly enthusiasm.

I remember the time when we wrote for *Focus*. Where did that enthusiasm go, man?

I'm rereading this letter and I must admire myself for my ability to depress the hell out of someone with my writing (that someone being a person who crossed the ocean to get treatment in America). What can one do? That's the way the things go around here. From another perspective, from another town (or continent), things in Zadar seem quite different. We Zadar people seem like lunatics to everybody else. Maybe that's not so far from the truth. Who here is still normal?

Listen, get in touch. I would be very glad if you did. And please write something for *Despite*. I have no idea what happened to Irena. *Really, whatever happened to Irena?* I usually don't get in touch with people who are not in Zadar. I simply don't know what to say to them.

Take care. You know what my mother used to say: "Get smart, Pavle!" And get well. A couple of fingers more or less, as if that matters? Anyway, what are fingers for anyway but for letting these trickles of happiness slip through them.

Bye.

31 March 1993

Dr. Marija Brida, a retired university professor, Croatian philosopher and humanist died in Jelsa on the island of Hvar. She spent most of her working life at the Faculty of Philosophy in Zadar. *It took a long, too long time to finally hold a commemoration for her at the Zadar faculty. Are some kind of ideological reasons at work? Or maybe worldviews?*

("I have a certain world view and I change my ideology every three years, which is normal. Therefore, I am not to blame: my ideology is at fault!" – this is the way people think today.)

Easter 1993 (*Despite* radio show)

INTRODUCTORY NOTE:

... What you have just heard was the poem "Jerusalem Dialogue" by Miroslav Krleža. The word for Easter [*Uskrs* in Croatian] is easily extracted from the word Despite [*Usprkos*]. Happy Easter and a peaceful day as well as the rest of the holidays.

This was an exclusive, occasional edition of *Despite*. If by any chance, despite the "rich" cultural life in Zadar, you are listening to this show, you are in the company of the long-haired, charming sound-woman Sandra (*Babac*), one of the most beautiful voices in Zadar and beyond – Gordana-Goga (*Baljak*) called *Georgia on my Mind*, and the wicked materialist (who does everything for a lot of money, or to be more precise: for free!), the witch and the editor of the show – Helena. If you enjoy such company, hang out with us for the next hour or so.

By the way, you have no idea how much we love you! That's right: you – who spend your Easter in this city that offers you so little comfort – who stay in your rooms beside your radio, not even watching television but cramming for the next exam and nibbling on your traditional Easter cakes. We love **you**, you who stayed here for Easter, in this town, that cannot be reached by electricity, but can be reached by the information that its cost will go up by 60 percent.

However, for every evil there is some good. Just think of all those new people whom you've met in these past two years while forced to wait in the line for brown bread or for water, or while passing salt sticks, playing *briškula*[29] or recapping the last episode of *Santa Barbara* in the basement (if you even go there!). (Have you noticed how the scenery of American soap operas includes massive high-quality doors?)

However, just as we wish you, our listeners, a Happy Easter, so the greeting has to go to our city, which is also going through a lot, just like its citizens. We have to wish it that its resurrection will happen as soon as possible.

Let us listen to Mahalia and *Happy Day* on this very day, on Easter, the same song we listened last time on our show while the city was being bombed. We listened to the song despite the shells. Because actually: no *Despite,* Easter or *Happy Day* is ever superfluous.

19 April 1993 (*Despite* radio show)

INTRODUCTION:

Good evening once again from another *Despite* show. We haven't heard from each other since Easter so there's a lot to be said tonight. I hope you will spend some time once again with our charming sound-woman Sandra, Ante (*Tomić*) and editor Helena. If by any chance you hear some strange sounds coming from the sky from the north-east during the show, don't get confused: they are just provocations. (For your consolation, what separates me from the north-east is just an open window.) The area between Zadar and Šibenik is just a neurotic region that allows itself to get provoked.

Besides, if they weren't mere provocations, someone would have dealt with those sounds long time ago, someone like Zagreb or the international community. And they are, naturally, smarter than us: they know what they're doing. Therefore: don't get provoked. This is, after all, the show called *DESPITE*.

INTRODUCTORY COMMENT: We witnessed various cultural events in Zadar from Easter till today. Three literary evenings held between the 14th and 16th of April at the Croatian Theatre House, a lecture by Prof. Ivo Banac, the premiere of the play *St Roko on the Hill*, the new play of the Zadar Puppet Theatre at the Days of Marul... So "who

---

[29] A popular card game in Dalmatia (pronounced "brishkula")

said that this town has disappeared?*"*, as a poet once asked. We will talk about all these events during the course of tonight's show.

And now, a few words about the things that *weren't* happening in Zadar in the past few days. On Tuesday 20th of April, the 59th international PEN congress (according to the President of PEN, Gyorg Konrad: it was, indeed, a congress) was held first in Hvar, but was then moved to Dubrovnik after many early problems, and it was attended by some 400 members from 30 countries. Many PEN centres did not send their representatives.

And so, due to the lack of a quorum, the congress couldn't be considered a working congress and so no revolutions – excuse me, resolutions – could be achieved. Many members couldn't attend it. The Russian writer, PEN member and greeeeat humanist, Limonov[30], couldn't come. And if he had come, he would have probably been joined by fellow writers and greeeeat humanists Vuk Drašković and Dobrica Ćosić[31]. Because they are humanists and the world's conscience. And thank heavens that in this case we don't have this kind of *pro-Serbian conscience* on our conscience. Let someone else take pride in such a *conscience*.

The distinguished authors travelled comfortably by ship from Venice to Hvar, and then to Dubrovnik on Wednesday, and after a cosy and pleasurable stay and arguments with each other on both land and sea, they comfortably returned to their homes. As if Fritz Beer had never warned that "an intellectually comfortable existence was an inevitable deathbed to ideas".

Let us remind ourselves that exactly sixty years ago, the 1933 PEN congress in Dubrovnik at the time of the rise of the Nazis, was attended by the famous British author and social prophet – Herbert George Wells. That same year, Wells became the president of world PEN, as the successor of the late John Galsworthy. It was that same Wells who predicted the future of the following thirty years in his 1909 article "The Possible Collapse of Civilisation". He saw the main causes for the world's coming to an end in too much armament and financial uncertainty, and once he said that modern warfare is madness and not a sound business proposition. He was also a man who anticipated science fiction of the contemporary type in his literary works. One of his such novels is *War of the Worlds*. In the sense of dollars deriving from it, it is important to mention that the famous movie

[30] Eduard Limonov, a strong supporter of the Serbs in the Yugoslav wars, notorious for being filmed firing a machine gun into Sarajevo at the invitation of the besieging Serbian forces

[31] Drašković and Ćosić are both writers from Serbia turned politicians.

Star Wars was modelled after it. If Mr. Wells were to rise from his grave by any chance, he would see that not even science fiction is what it used to be, that the kind of science fiction he used to write is now covered in dust, and that in these parts of the world fantastic wars of the worlds occurred, which he couldn't have even imagined.

We wish the PEN members a pleasant return home. Despite the war of the worlds.

SIGNING OFF: And so we come to the end of another show of *Despite.* The students who usually tune in with their own contributions have obviously prolonged their Easter holidays a bit. I know, this place is getting more and more *uncomfortable* to live in. But we are here despite all of it. Maybe it will get better by our next show. I mean, less uncomfortable.

Before the end of this show, I have to thank Sandra and Ante for putting up with me. All the best from your editor and radio host with my usual greeting: Even if we mean stars made of projectiles – walk tall under the stars!

According to the number of newspapers that were published in Croatian towns and villages up to 1920, Zadar holds second place, right after Zagreb. There were as many as 82 papers just in Croatian, and more of them published in Italian, German and Latin. In almost 150 years, 147 to be precise, including two interwar periods, Zadar published or is still publishing 112 papers in Croatian. That is a substantial number, which would be even greater if it hadn't been for the Treaty of Rapallo, which forbade any kind of publishing activities in Zadar for as long as 21 years.

7 May 1993

I'm fascinated by the thought that one needs to be just a few hundred miles north-west or west of here to live completely differently. To be free from the binary air we are currently breathing: one moment you're there, the next you're gone. How is it possible that simple geography determines the most elementary existence?

8 May 1993

Mirko Bogović's play *Stephen, the Last King of Bosnia* was premiered last night in Zadar, performed by the Puppet Theatre ensemble. Tomislav Durbešić, the director, wrote the following to mark the occasion: "I'm not saying that this tragedy of Bogović is either good or bad, but it does have undeniable worth: it traces, for that period, the hard search to express in the early Croatian language all the secrets of language and human beings." The director also found certain advantages of this text when drawing analogies between the events that occurred in Bosnia in the 15th century and what is going on today. Therefore, we must congratulate our small but worldly Puppet Theatre on this play, which everyone was hoping to watch in one piece, without interruptions from shells. (*The play was performed only twice because during a shelling soon afterwards, its expensive costumes and masks were stolen from its storage room inside the Church of St Dominic.*) For now, we can say that the Zadar Puppet Theatre, Durbešić and Mihatov accomplished, if not an objectively grand play, then at least an important performance whose worth cannot be measured simply by a theatrical yardstick.

9 June 1993

"In our Zadar daily routine, which mostly lasts until 2 pm, in which many important things have lost their meaning, in which death itself – however frequent, or precisely because it is so frequent – becomes just a dry statement, tonight we will once again listen about the little details, the meanings resting in the forgotten particles of existence, in the blinking candles (human) which remain lit and will not go off, by some miracle, even when surrounded with noisy and shiny pyrotechnics. Therefore, even though he is in this time and space, the individual remains just a historical pattern and brought by his predictability to the vulgarity of cliché, we still manage to meet during a poetry night..."

Two hours after I spoke those words at the presentation of the newest poetry collection by a poet from Zadar, I was sitting in the company of some ten "poetry lovers" on the terrace of the Fish restaurant in Zadar's Foša. The night was clear, and the sky full of stars. A night, so it seemed, like any early summer night in Zadar. The chit-chatting and laughing of the company, partly fuelled by wine, was suddenly interrupted by the hissing of some other stars that were flying above us and fell into the sea, just some hundred metres away. And as if this wasn't such an unpleasant surprise, we perceived this Russian roulette as some sort of very original fun. I phoned my parents from the restaurant. They were very upset, especially because Rapunzel, due to my professional-artistic-unpaid engagement that evening, had to spend the night at my parent's apartment, on the south-eastern side of the seventh floor of a "skyscraper" in the most exposed block in the city – so they requested that I return home immediately.

I stayed with the company for a bit longer (after I'd calmed my parents down by saying that "nothing especially bad was going to happen"). Driving home alone to Voštarnica in my *peglica*[32], I didn't feel any fear

[32] Literally meaning "a small iron"; a nickname for a Fiat 126, held to look like an

(even though the shells "had me on a plate"): I recalled similar situations when during classes, around midday, the "stars" would fall into the sea right next to our faculty building, situated on the "most beautiful waterfront in the world", while the "most insane students in the world" listened to lectures held by me and my colleagues. In such situations, when I was at my parents, usually during lunch in the kitchen turned towards the "sun and the stars", Rapunzel would quickly come down from her chair (on which she would sit "on her heels"), grab her plate from the table and run, with her short legs dressed in wide trousers, towards the living room, supposedly the "safest"[33] room in the apartment, place her plate on the table and continue eating deliciously. As if nothing had happened.

2 October 1993
Sweet Irma (to a girl from Sarajevo)

"..." – said the dog and extinguished a lead cigar on Irma's back.

"Don't ask me anything, child" – mother had told her a moment earlier.

The dog puffs out some smoke, and no one asked mother about anything any more.

11 November 1993

It was about ten in the evening. The shells were hissing and flying over the bus, like falling stars.

"Make a wish," I whisper to myself.

No one knew I was on the way. I was approaching a town during an alert. I hope no one on the bus recognizes me, I thought.

False love and war – a shallow but tangible metaphor for Eros and Thanatos.

I needed it. A hug. After several hours, I was lying with my back turned to him. I felt strong, supreme even. I got what I wanted: a mirage of warmth and closeness. Without kisses, naturally: because they disgusted me. I felt a relief at the thought of returning home in the morning, incognito. Because: I was returning home. To a city during an alert.

28 November 1993
Wind and the Last of the Mohicans (*Narodni List*)[34]

Mr. Daniel V.[35] benevolently expects an article. Mister Daniel Day-

---

iron

[33] During the war in Zadar, as it turned out no building or room was ever safe: people were killed even in their basements.

[34] *Narodni List* is a newspaper issued in Zadar.

[35] "Daniel V." is in fact Danijel Vučenović who was at that time the editor-in-chief

Lewis plays the last of the Mohicans. But let's start from the beginning.

We started from the beginning. The fellowship of the "Special Drive" departed at midnight on November 26th to the "Days of Zadar" in Zagreb, and the bus took aboard several soldiers who were on their way to Maslenica. Among them was a 23-year-old draftee with a pirate look, a headscarf on his head, from Split. Once I would have called him Mandrilo[36], but I won't now. He told me how, when he was at home in Split with his wife and children, he wanted to go back to the front as soon as possible. He doesn't want to do anything else as long as the war lasts. The only problem is, as he said, that others don't care enough about what people like him were doing, sneaking into enemy villages at night, not knowing whether they will ever return. I'm not sure if he believed me when I said that I appreciated what he was doing. I didn't ask his name on purpose. He could have been called Goliath or David, or Roland – whatever. The Split guy left the bus. Went into the night. God knows… I thought, but didn't want to finish the thought.

* * *

So, "Days of Zadar" at the Croatian Heritage Foundation in Zagreb. Or a trip down a blocked road to the capital. It seemed as if the road leading to it was more blocked that we expected. First, as we crossed the pontoon a bit after midnight – most of us for the first time in our lives – in the extremely well-equipped bus, we watched on video a documentary on the destruction of Zadar. The bus driver later explained: "To remind ourselves". I wonder however, whether this film about Zadar during the war was ever shown on that final night of the "Days of Zadar". I suppose people there need no reminders. In Karlobag, while we waited for the unblocking of the road and the blessing of the traffic warden, and while the bus was swinging relentlessly in ice and wind, we watched a movie entitled *Wind*. I guess, again, to remind ourselves...

* * *

They say that the final night of the showbiz-poetic creativity of undefeated wartime Zadar was – a success. Zadar is a city of dignified people. Who will never admit defeat.

---

of *Narodni List.*

[36] A pejorative nickname used by other Dalmatians for an inhabitant of Split; from the Italian *mandrillo*, meaning a mandrill or, colloquially, a lecher

In Zagreb, all these dignified people were welcomed with eyes full of pity and understanding, so to say. The way you look at traumatized, abandoned, asocial children who might do something unpredictable, make a scene.

Such children should not be taken seriously in the end. And you have to forgive them (the children). I don't know if anyone mentioned the number of seven suicides in Zadar in the past month. If not, I suppose the reason for this lies in the danger of possible disruption of the showbiz-poetic concept of presenting a city that has remained in high spirits over the past few years.

I remember an article about visiting Zagreb, which was published some two years ago. Little has changed. Except maybe the fact that at that time they wrote about the destroyed bridge and now they will write about the pontoon.

Zagreb was and remained distant. The road to and from Zagreb was blocked. For example, it wasn't simple to cross the square next to the railway station. There, in front of King Tomislav, a multi-floored building was being built underground. Brick by brick. Brick of doubt for potential regionalists, autonomists, anti-centralists. A challenge to irascible, disobedient people from Dalmatia who obediently stay in Dalmatia. However, they don't allow themselves to be provoked by an underground architectural miracle whose top will consist of flowers instead of a roof.

On our way to Zadar, we watched the rest of the movie about the destruction in and around Zadar. In the late afternoon on the Senj–Karlobag road, things seemed very bleak. The hilltops by the road were covered in clouds. As if cigarette smoke was pumping through the bus windows and covering the hills. In the distance we could see a name sign on a tavern. The screen was showing bodies of people from Škabrnja covered in black plastic sheeting.

"Lunch!" said Tome cheerfully. I flinched. A thorn in the eye. "Lunch... lunch... lunch...!" echoing in my head. Škabrnja. A limping dog next to our parked bus. Cigarette smoke still covers the clouds. Be merciful, don't add anything...

After most of us satisfied our hunger and thirst, the video showed the movie *The Last of the Mohicans*. Daniel Day-Lewis, the Hamlet from pre-war Lovrijenac[37] and son of Cecyl, English author of beautiful war poetry lines (if one can write about war in a beautiful way) – was Hawk Eye. The dark-haired, bony Mohican or Hamlet turned away from Uncle Ivan's house in Rovanjska, the house whose eyes were poked out. The holes

[37] A fortress standing on a cliff just outside Dubrovnik, where *Hamlet* is traditionally played every year

where windows once stood are now dark sockets. When Uncle Ivan, Mate and Ante return to Rovanjska and Novigrad, it might be good to return with them. To heal the wounds of the mutilated houses. To bring them their sight back. I don't think we'll plant flowers on the roofs of the houses.

Finally, we cross the pontoon. For the second time in my life. It's no shiny Golden Gate, but it's ours, it's the darkened war bridge of hope. Our trip to Zagreb lasted fifteen hours, but our return was considerably shorter: only nine and a half hours. Our bus will be the only one leaving the capital that night.

* * *

Mr. Daniel V. got his article. Mr. Daniel Day-Lewis played the last of the Mohicans. Our bus drove to the city lights of the true capital in northern Dalmatia.

We were going back. We – irascible, bitter, dignified people.

The last of the Mohicans.

JELE[38]

17 December 1993

From time to time I throw myself back on my landlord's (too) big double bed with old springs, and I lie still in the twilight of the room, staring at its ceiling, lit only by candlelight. Ema is in the next room, the dining room, in the middle of a pile of toys scattered across the old shabby carpet. War, loneliness, cold, a child with a questionable future in the next room... I feel my throat clenching.

Today (you see, how interesting), as if the bitterness is somewhere on the brim of the gullet similar to that of old times. I feel sick to my stomach from all those patriotic and similar hypocrites. I wish to keep quiet and not blabber nonsense in order to keep my head above water, getting ideas how all that hesitation has any sense...

Fuck you all.

18 December 1993

Tower of Babylon (*Narodni List*)

"You wanted to, admit it!"

"I admit it..."

"You wanted to do something for this City?"

"I did..."

"You wanted to raise the dead?"

"I did..."

---

[38] "JELE" was my pen name in Zadar newspaper *Narodni list.*

"You wanted to play Jesus a bit, didn't you?"
The Enthusiast shrugs his shoulders:
"I did."
"Well than play Christ till the end!"
The Devil exits slamming the door behind him.
The Enthusiast stays alone. As always.

* * *

Once there was a City. In it lived Enthusiasts and those who weren't. The Enthusiasts decided to build a tower that would reach the skies. They asked a Non-Enthusiast for help. But since the Enthusiasts and Non-Enthusiasts spoke in different languages, they couldn't understand each other. The Enthusiasts' language was their ideas, the Non-Enthusiasts' was money and power. The Enthusiasts thought that there was a wish for new ideas in the Non-Enthusiasts' heads, but the Non-Enthusiasts – even though they beat their chests to show their loyalty to new ideas – were convinced that the Enthusiasts only wanted money and power. One side projected its own mechanisms of thinking onto the other. Gradually, tension built up between them. Envy and competition rose both among the Enthusiasts and those who weren't. Good ideas were cut off at the root. Also, friendships withered away and animosity spread without mercy. The City was on the verge of disaster. (That same City had withstood both plagues and wars and famine for centuries.)

Suddenly there was shouting in the City: the Enthusiasts expressed their ideas, the Non-Enthusiasts pointed their finger at the exchange rate and slammed their fist on the table. Finally, there was panic, and the city, after thousands of years of its existence, was wiped off the face of the earth. The tower was never built.

The City's name **wasn't** Babylon.

* * *

"You wanted to, admit it!" the Devil screamed.
"I did..." said the Enthusiast.
"The Devil wouldn't leave you alone..."
The Enthusiast stands up and, slamming the door behind him, leaves the City.

JELE

23 December 1993 (Christmas edition of *Narodni List*)
So It Is If You Think So [39]

"Good morning, dear listeners. The crew of our radio station wishes you a merry Christmas and reminds you that today is the two-hundred-and-forty-somethingth day of the general alert..."

The editors call this section (without my knowing let alone my permission) "Mirror of Reality" (Pirandello is probably turning in his grave because of this title). With all due respect to the person who chose this title, I must say that I am astounded. First of all, because I don't like mirrors; secondly, as for reality – I'm not in the clear about what reality actually is. But, since many wise men weren't quite clear about mimesis either, starting with Aristotle to Auerbach (I leave the living alone, because one mustn't speak ill of the living) – I conclude that it is not my place to be clear. I reserve therefore the right to my own version of reality and its projections. Also, I want to warn those of you who are not clear about reality and are surrounded by those convinced that they are, it can easily rebound on you. But that's for some other story. Or even rebound on your head.

Recently, a man from Zadar, although not "from Zadar" any more since he left the City sometime ago looking for a better living (or living for a better look), said that "up here it is almost the same as in Zadar; the only difference is that there's no shooting there". At first I thought I misunderstood him, but then I realized I – hadn't. The man said this pretty casually, almost consolingly. This classic line was pronounced so convincingly that I immediately thought: "It's true, the man is right. Well it is the same, there's no difference." But then a post scriptum appears in your mind saying: "There's no difference especially when you consider that this man – left Zadar." And then I realized that my own reality was very different from the reality of that particular gentleman.

While I was ending this last sentence, I heard something whizz by and hit something. Not in the hinterland or in the suburbs but here. Maybe somewhere near that exact same swing in the playground in Jazine[40] or that theatre fence where some children might have played with Lego this morning or watched a Christmas play. Here somewhere, very near. Here, in the head, inside the chest. One of my colleagues once said to me how everything looked quite simple when you consider physics. From the moment you hear something fired, count for some three seconds. That's how much time you have. It's nothing. If the first one doesn't hit you, and you manage to hide in those three seconds, there's not much chance that

[39] A play by the Italian writer Luigi Pirandello (1867-1936)
[40] A district of Zadar

the second one will hit you. It can all be quite simply put. Everything can be rationalized. This whiz was just an ordinary sound of mass and speed. It's nothing. Boom and dust – they are a natural, physical consequence of impact or rather strength. If the problem is rationalized, there is actually not much of mental and emotional energy for fear, anxiety, for expectation that has been piling up for the past three years, for anger... And don't let me even get started on love and hate (if you hate somebody, God forbid). Three years of war condensed into three seconds of your chance for survival. Pure physics. It's nothing.

* * *

It's almost Christmas, the day for forgiveness and holy gifts of love. I remember the words from one of my acquaintances: "It's the same up there..." It's very simple, they say, this reality of ours. It can be explained by physics. It doesn't produce malice or envy, it doesn't expect condolence. However, in our reality the lights in the window sparkle (if there is electricity) differently from those up there – where it's the same. Here the kids in Jazine swing differently from those up there – where it's the same. Here, a child's hug and a handshake during Christmas Eve Mass are different than there – where it's the same. Therefore I think that something is missing from this scientific explanation: our sentimentality cannot be explained by physical laws. Nor can physics explain our Christmas.

Merry *our* Christmas, dear citizens of Zadar.

Even if it is – the way it seems to you.

JELE

3 January 1994

It is here... (*Narodni List*)

At the beginning of this article as well as of the New Year, I owe our readers an apology on behalf of our printers – both the current and the former ones – for all those printing mistakes they have had to endure in previous issues of *Narodni List*. One such example was the Christmas article in this section. It is interesting to note the power of such supposedly unimportant "typos": they can change the author's "general description" in an instant, his world view and even ethnic affiliation. Let alone the grotesque semantic/syntactic combinations and allusions that come out of those printing gremlins. With this apology, I send my New Year's wishes to our typesetters and may they become ever better at their work in the years to come.

* * *

So it has arrived. Ten years after Orwell's *1984*, it is here, the mysterious, sparkling with suspense, brand new – 1994. All of us have entered this year with best wishes for themselves and their loved ones, leaving behind that sickness of unavoidable recapitulation that overcomes us during the Christmas and New Year's holidays, recapitulation of everything that was done and accomplished – or not – in the past year.

* * *

For some people, New Year's Eve started with a cocktail party organized by *Narodni List* at the restaurant Marina. The unexpectedly high number of guests was, frankly speaking, more terrifying than impressive. The feeling it induced could have been summed up in a question: who is going to pay for all of this? Maybe even the author of this article could have been counted as one of the excess guests, because she rudely expected something else from the party, or rather from the guests. The party itself, the dinner and the programme were quite decent, because, naturally, people need some kind of occasion from time to time to cheer them up or at least suppress the unease induced by warfare. However, one could occasionally hear some unbelievable remarks in the department of the surplus. For example, those too well accustomed to the comforts of their home or those who miss those comforts very much noticed how they couldn't possibly drink wine served from anything other than a 70 cl bottle. Those who were currently occupying Croatian hotels not as guests but as homeless refugees would probably have no problem with drinking wine from a one-litre bottle on this New Year's Eve. And so the evening in the honour of the Balkans' oldest weekly couldn't possibly have gone by without lucid Balkan remarks. But, maybe we should treat them as the "typos" of the evening. There was also talk about people that night – about women rather than men – so one could conclude that a person needs only a few days without shelling to start talking more or less convincingly about people they know barely or not at all. Some talked about work, some even gave out their business cards eagerly. Some laughs, some cursing... That evening, it was obvious that the men, in their falsely casual businessmen roles, tried to be men, and women, extras as usual, tried to be women. Too many guests and yet, as it seems, too few men and too few women.
And so arrived the year that is expected to be New.

JELE

23 January 1994

"Victory" of the Brothers Lumiere (*Narodni List*)

Whenever I thought of the *Pobjeda* (Victory) cinema, to be honest, I was never quite sure which victory was in question.

I went to the cinema on Saturday. For the first time since the war began, I went to a Zadar cinema, to the only cinema, *Pobjeda*. On my way there, I thought about *Cyrano* at the cinema *Zadar* that was featured at the beginning of war with three and a half people in the audience (one of them was asleep). Not even the gifted big-nose Depardieux was funny enough for the citizens of Zadar back then. I suppose men who have spirit and who unselfishly and generously write love letters under a false name have been out of fashion for a long time.

And yet, my recent venture to the cinema represented a huge breakthrough for me. In fact, it was a somewhat bizarre adventure. It took some courage to do that: after all those student pilgrimages to Zagreb cinemas like the charming *Jadran*, intellectual *Kinoteka*, fancy *Studio* and the Baroque *Balkan*, which was renamed *Europa* a few years ago (maybe because of that Latin saying: *Nomina sunt odiosa*). It took some courage to do that, as I said. Because the auditorium of the *Pobjeda*, too dark to be considered lit, was more like a hall of dubious morals than of a cultural institution of such a grand name. This building should be famous! Next year, we celebrate the hundredth anniversary of the first public cinematographic projection in the world. "But, this is a war zone," someone will reply. And this is not Paris, I am aware of that. Within those ten metres that separated me from the lady who checks the tickets at the entrance, I thought about how someone should donate a few light bulbs to the cinema so that at least the pathway leading to the Hollywood illusion would be illuminated. The movie was wonderful: the images were moving so fast that you couldn't quite "catch" all the jokes of Disney's students. The colours from the big screen lit up all the little and big faces in the seats of our small (provincial?) cinema, like the ones from neo-realistic Italian black-and-white movies in which there is at least one local fool waddling about or at least one heaving chesty lady of dubious generosity.

It was a fairytale. Aladdin and Jasmine conquered the mean wizard and got married. Later on, they had many children so they paid less income tax. And all this with the help of a magic lamp and its muscular genie who in the end, to complete the overall joy, earns back his freedom. And everything would have been wonderful if someone's cynical dad hadn't noticed on our way out of the cinema that Aladdin was – a Muslim.

Ah, and I thought for a second there how great it would be to own that rusty magic lamp and ask the genie to make our only cinema into a place a bit worthier of the Lumière brothers. With just a few more light bulbs and a few buckets of yellow paint for the doors and doorposts. Maybe we could use *Pobjeda* to defeat all those boring and stupefying TV and video boxes that are transforming from pets into family bosses. But this is not Paris, I know.

Nevertheless, one day we might achieve *Victory*.

JELE

30 January 1994
Reincarnation

When I entered the courtyard of Dubrovnik's Inter-University Centre one afternoon, Chester Beers, an American of Croatian descent whose age was impossible to determine, stood leaning on the concrete fence in front of the building. He said that he'd overestimated his physical abilities and was dead tired. He probably decided that I kept my further enquiries to myself due to politeness, so Ches explained that the capacity of his lungs was rather small because they were completely destroyed due to toxic gas inhalation during the war. The Vietnam War.

My amazement by the fact a fragile man like Beers participated in some kind of war was heightened by the view, which I had up until then, that war was some sort of collective evil that lay forgotten in the dusty drawers of the past and which came to life from time to time in movies and books. I didn't know much more about war. And then this Ches shows up, an American nothing like those tanned compatriots of his with big bellies and chequered trousers who patiently wait for their wife's luggage at the airport.

It was not until someone with a mutilated body showed up, someone who couldn't breath or walk like other people and whose powerlessness was grotesque when compared to the fairytale suburbia decorated with giant blooming agaves – it was not until then that my understanding of reality could grasp some kind of perception about what it really means and stands for – WAR.

"In August 1967, Chester Beers became a 100 percent invalid. His mother's parents were Croats who came to America in 1913. Ches was born in California, but started living in Oregon after the war. In 1985, he survived an almost fatal attack of pneumonia and dedicated the rest of his life to writing poetry and his craving for travelling. He travelled across America, Canada and Europe, finally visiting his grandfather's homeland, where he stayed the most..." (From the introduction of his manuscript.)

Ches wrote odes to Dubrovnik, Hvar, the Adriatic… At times, he seemed to overdo it in his enthusiasm. The things that he could breathe into with the full *remains* of his lungs seemed ordinary and everyday to me. He also wrote about his war buddies.

After that time in Dubrovnik, we met once again: in Zagreb. He gave me the manuscript of his poetry collection. He wanted me to translate it. So that he might publish it, here in Croatia. After that, I received a few of his letters. The last letter I received was my own, which had a "Deceased" stamp on it.

In the autumn of 1991, the Inter-University Centre in Dubrovnik was hit by a shell. Chester Beers, wherever you are, know that the new Saigon played right out here. And Da Nang. And Hue...[41]

* * *

Fever is a nasty thing. It won't let you concentrate on anything. I'm lying in my bed, staring across the cover through the unbelievably pink curtains and window glass strapped with sellotape (so it won't shatter from explosions!) at the laundry relentlessly swinging back and forth on the balcony clothes dryer. Like Villon's hanged bodies behind the see-through sentimentality.

I found the name of a friend
I had known in High School
On the Black Wall,
And then I found another.
I looked for my own name
But it was not there.[42]

31 January 1994 (*Narodni List*)
"After the War" – in quotation marks

Formally. We can also shake hands formally. With a person we've just met, with a friend or – an enemy. Enemy of the state, I mean. Who bombarded us, who killed us, forced us to live a bare existence without electricity, water, road connections. We listened carefully to the midnight news on a worn-out radio with used-up batteries because of that same enemy. We used to freeze when the doors of someone's car banged because of that same enemy. We used to walk the Zadar streets in the

---

[41] "Reincarnation" in the title refers to the never-ending series of "reincarnations" in the bodies of war invalids. Invalids of any war.
[42] Verses from Beers' poem *My Umbrella*

middle of the day longing for that pseudo-political (because no one really knows anything about politics!) conversation with our friend over coffee, or at least for that half hour to go by in peace.

And yet, despite all that, many of us went to exhibition openings, book promotions, concerts at Donat. During the shelling and the destruction. While people were being killed. We used every opportunity to silence the spiritual fasting that was imposed on us. We forced life. Or the appearance of a life. We were proud, bitter, pathetic...

But after all that, "after the war" (with or without quotation marks), always follows, naturally, the burying of the hatchet. There follows the peace when you light candles for the dead but also turn new pages, make plans, meet people. Shake hands with people. With friends. With enemies. Formally. Like at the beginning of the story. *They say that Ceca (wasn't she Arkan's sweetheart?)*[43] *will hold a concert soon in the middle of Zagreb.*

And yet, I beg those shaking hands with the latter to spare me their ear-to-ear smile; Vukovar, Škabrnja and everything else that still lies in the ruins in Croatia was not a result of some courtyard fight between two offended boys. Truly, leave me at least so much Croatian, or better yet, Zadar dignity so I don't have to – smile...

JELE

20 March 1994

Two days ago, we entered into confederation with Bosnia. Yesterday, so I've heard, some shells fell near the motel situated on the edge of Biograd. The pontoon is their frequent target.

Despite all that, Zadar is coming back to life.

I'm still scared. In the past months: mostly of loneliness. "Mister", so I heard, got married in December.

9 April 1994

It seems as if in the past months I simply radiate with loneliness. It is materialized in confusion, being torn apart, weariness. I received today one of the first copies of *Glasje*. Our journal.

20 December 1994

Recently, I was told the following by Davor Ž., who left Zadar some 15 years ago and who will most likely spent the rest of his life in the

[43] Željko Ražnjatović Arkan was a Serbian career criminal and later a paramilitary leader; he was notorious for committing massacres in Bosnia during the war in the former Yugoslavia during the nineties.

(domestic or foreign) diaspora: "Don't do anything publicly in Zadar. Let them be: simply do whatever you do for yourself and don't fight the windmills. Any kind of work in Zadar apart from private business is a complete nonsense."

19 January 1995

It has arrived. This morning. In a pistachio-coloured envelope. With Elisabeth's head in the corner. A letter. Civilized. Almost scented. From Snježana. Still unopened. Lying there, on the table, since this morning.

* * *

In the autumn of 1991, fluorescent posters on the London underground seemed as though they would come off and fall from the wall. The new album of the Irish singer Van Morrison, the Nobel Prize for Literature went to Nadine Gordimer (Republic of South Africa), a new movie entitled *Object of Beauty* (starring John Malkovich, and Glenn Close starring in a movie with some banal title)... Followed by a poster with a shocking question: "How is it to be raped at the age of 3?" An array of casualness, carefreeness, (false) compassion, western sentimentality...

What are the miles that separate you from me, me from you, Snježana? Miles of space? Miles of experience?

* * *

The letter remains unopened to this day. It is probably lying in some drawer. I think it will stay that way. Snježana, sorry, you have nothing to say to me. Nor do I to you.

Nothing of importance. *Ništa važno*.

* * *

God, I wish I lived differently. Too many people believe that others should live according to their rules. I try to catch some daylight. I can't sing "Moja do-mo-vi-na" (*My Homeland*) with Rapunzel. My voice won't leave my throat.

20 January 1995
Syndrom Iadertinum (*Narodni List*)

It seems that the citizens of Zadar find it hard to send their voice beyond the city limits. The reasons must be of a political nature, into which very few want or can go.

That's why citizens of Zadar usually let others form their ideas about life in this town. During the past few (war) years, three-minute clips on the central news usually came down to the numbers of the dead and wounded. (The living and the survivors were not of particular importance to the media.) Once in a while, some kind of documentary would appear on the TV – such as *Golden and Silver Zadar* (financed by local sources) by the author who will forever be dubbed as "Nomina sunt odiosa" – offering a fragmentary and, I would say, superficial way of presenting the "real picture" of what was happening in Zadar in the past years. Curiously enough, for the filming of the aforementioned documentary, the electricity supply was cut off from the Zadar Peninsula[44] for a few hours in order to shoot "memorable" *chiaro-scuro* scenes with faces above candles, like those in Michelangelo Caravaggio's paintings. Ever since I watched that movie, I can't stop wondering: where were these filmmakers when Zadar really didn't have electricity for months? (Therefore, the banknotes will never feature the symbol of Zadar. An image of a generator is inappropriate because it evokes ugly memories.)

The "cherry on the cake" can sometimes be bitter, as was confirmed by the recent visit of a certain Intellectual to Zadar, a very "broad" person (in the functional sense) from Croatian National Television, on the occasion of possible reopening of a television studio in this city. At a press conference, the Intellectual described his attitude towards Zadar, its citizens, its journalists, athletes, pedagogues (basically towards many things, as can be expected from a choleric *uomo universale* who seems to have been educated and brought up according to the speedy "comic method", and has accordingly taken up politics, "passing" his judgement fiercely on both things he should and shouldn't.) To say that this gentleman from National Television was spreading insults and slanders about Zadar wartime and post-war everyday life – would be a mere euphemism. To call it humiliation would be a poor choice of words considering that this humiliation was preceded by another one, which has lasted all these war years and is officially called a "general alert".

---

[44] Zadar was founded on a small peninsular, and the old part of town is simply referred to by locals as "the Peninsular".

But: "every miracle lasts three days"[45]. "Excess situations" go by quickly; logically and psychologically justified protest turned to simple complaints that are being digested, like some digestive before a meal, on the National Square, in the company of friends, with hands in pockets – basically nothing.

Such behaviour might seem interesting to an observer and maybe it will be written down in medical lexica as the "Zadar Syndrome" (Syndrom Iadertium). In layman's terms, it could be explained as follows: if someone spits in your face, turn the other cheek. So they can spit at you once again.

JELE

12 February 1995

This morning, around 4 am, a bomb exploded in the market; it was placed under one of the news-stands, so they say. At the moment of the explosion, a policeman standing next to the news-stand in question was seriously injured. Jasenka, who accompanied me to the cinema, wouldn't share this news with me up until after the (excellent) movie *Forrest Gump*, when we went to Mozaik for drinks.

This is only one of the events with a similar turn that have happened in Zadar in the past months. A bit before Christmas, during lunch break, at the Technical High School one of the students blew himself to pieces, which were found a kilometre away from the explosion.

We, who remain after such events, are becoming more and more numb towards violent death and suicides, which have become daily occurrences.

When all this is over, I will most definitely have no time for my own foolishness and other people's obscenities.

7 April 1995

Today we had the opportunity to see the premiere of the play *Zvjezdan* (*The Star-Child*), performed by actors of the Zadar Puppet Theatre. The play was based on a dramatization of the story written by the English author, advocate of "art for art's sake", Oscar Wilde at the beginning of this century. It was a story about good and evil, which keep changing like yin and yang. Mr Dundov successfully transformed the story which is a good example of Wilde's paradoxical and grotesque literature. One starry evening, a forester finds a boy called Zvjezdan in the woods, and takes him in to bring him up in his poor but large family. Despite the kindness and nobleness of the people surrounding him, Zvjezdan represents the true image of evil; he spreads evil wherever he can, even when he encounters

[45] Croatian folk saying

his real, old and poor mother. He is punished for his wickedness by being turned from a beautiful boy with golden hair into an unwelcome scarecrow, tortured and avoided by everyone.

However, Zvjezdan receives the order from the king to find a lost treasure. Despite many difficulties, he finds the treasure but decides to give it to a beggar. After numerous troubles, Zvjezdan is – like in any fairytale – finally rewarded: he gets back his beautiful looks, becomes the heir to the throne because of his generosity and finally admits that his mother and the beggar are his parents. The puppets in this play remind me of those Polish theatre animations by Jelenia Góra, who featured the *Wardrobe* at last year's PIF[46], a play based on the poem by Guillaume Apollinaire and the fairytale *The Steadfast Tin Soldier* by Hans Christian Andersen.

In another work by Wilde, *Dorian Gray*, as I can remember, the central character also said he thought that it was better to be beautiful than good. I think about the duality of the same person, about beauty seen as the physical manifestation of evil, and ugliness as a reflection of goodness and nobleness, or about ugliness as the punishment for sins, about Wilde's aesthetics of the English Secession...

I think about good and evil embodied within the same person, fascinated by beauty that could simply be a cover-up of evil and cruelty, about the aesthetics in which one looks for the good. Monstrosity disguised or covered up by beauty, monstrosity that takes its real form in atrocity and disgust. Searching for both the good and the beautiful within the same grotesque figure.

Is *Zvjezdan* a fairy story for grown-ups? A fairy story, so they say, is didactic literature that teaches children the existence of good and evil, beautiful and monstrous, yin and yang, abstract corruption of the spirit, sin disguised as beauty. In them vice and virtue are subject matters for a work of art.

Do we need a fairy story at this moment in order to believe in the existence of good?

27 April 1995

I drove to Biograd. I almost crashed my dad's car by overtaking a car on a bend. A close call. Mum's return from her examination in Zagreb: mild collagenosis.

---

[46] International Festival of Puppet Theatre, an annual event held in Zagreb

5 May 1995

Together with my students and some actors from the Zadar Puppet Theatre (*Zlatko, Dragan, Anđela – the jewels of Croatian puppetry...)*, I'm working at the small theatre in Jazine on a scenic collage entitled *Colleague, the War Is On for Too Long...* based on a dramatization of my own texts, published in *Narodni List* during 1992 and 1993 under the pseudonym "Jele", and on some texts I read on the radio show *Despite*. A few days ago, during the bombing of Zagreb, a talented student of direction, named Luka Skračić, was wounded. It's still uncertain if he will live or not. (*"Sometimes it seems to me that I will lose my mind from all the pain", I was told recently by my colleague Vlado, father of the late Luka, shortly after it happened, while we were crossing the Zadar Bridge.*) Some of the students working with me on this play are his cousins. *The war really is lasting too long.*

20 May 1995 (*Narodni List*)

- - - It seems that the citizens of Zadar find it hard to send their voice beyond the city limits. The reasons must be of a political nature, into which very few want or can go.

That's why citizens of Zadar usually let others form their ideas about life in this town. During the past few (war) years, three-minute clips on the central news usually came down to numbers of the dead and wounded. The living and the survivors are (were) not of particular importance to the media. Maybe that's why the banknotes will never feature the symbol of Zadar. An image of an aggregate is inappropriate because it evokes ugly memories. - - -

JELE

28 July 1995

The Point of the Theatre (*Narodni List*)

Congratulations, Davor! That's what everyone who knows Davor Žagar, the director and adapter of Kušan's theatre play *The Point of Freedom*, should say to him with respect after seeing his show.

Overwhelmed by impressions after the play based on Kušan's drama *The Point of Freedom*, it is hard to find any words. By giving the historical overview of a "free" city, history that is being sold out (because history – is destiny), the Auctioneer counts in the Lucipherian-Šerbedžijan[47] manner: Going once... going twice... And each new auction, each new sale is actually a reliving of the same cycle of one's own History, from which

[47] A word derived from the family name of the Croatian-American actor Rade Šerbedžija; pronounced as "Sherbegian"

one never learns, on the contrary, which he tries to silence. Porphirogenet, the leader of the Pirates, the Venetians and French, or even Ferdinand – is just sleezy/violent/pointless/degeneric etc. Variation on the theme of a ruler – who was (re)incarnated with bravura by Slavko Jaruga. Gundulić's[48] "The wheel of fortune spins..." gets its finale in Žagar's adaptation: who wants down, down (they) stay. Today it's the "Wheel of Fortune" with Tanja Tušek, and among the winnings are: the French, Venetians, Turks, Austrians or maybe ice-cream, *burek*[49] (with pilchards)... maybe even *čevapčići*[50]. But what ever way you turn it, you get owned by someone else.

And when Grace(iela) finally appears, the young woman who appears during the show like some Diogenes or a character from the *Divine Comedy*, whose head appears from the mud, the woman who saved her virginity for Frane but then lost it to a Turk, finds new hope because she will regain her virginity at the source of the river Zrmanja. This is how Žagar foresees the destiny of the one in whose honour today (first) songs are sung, because of whom men sat in prisons, the one they wish to sell out. During the war? You bet, when best if not during the war. (Sale first, than transformation[51] – so we won't complain later that we didn't know.)

Each new reading will surely give another meaning to this show. Žagar gathered a young ensemble from the Acting Studio and set in motion all of their potential, freeing them to scream, to laugh, to sing. I think, we should all thank him for it.

28 August 1995

A moment ago, I saw images of a morning slaughter at the Sarajevo market. They said that around 11 am, a shell fell onto the market killing thirty-two victims, mostly children, women and old people. In the past four or five years, since this new Balkan slaughterhouse opened its doors, I think I still haven't learned to view death as a collective number where individual tragedy is of no importance. I haven't learned a thing.

---

[48] Ivan Gundulić – a Croatian Baroque poet

[49] A type of baked or fried filled pastry, popular in the Arab world and throughout the Balkans

[50] Skinless grilled mixed meat sausages, very popular in Croatia and other countries in the region

[51] A reference to Croatia's "privatisation and transformation" in which many of Croatia's state-owned companies were transferred to private ownership, often in less than transparent circumstances, and then underwent "transformation" to market-oriented enterprises

This morning, for the first time in four whole years, I heard the voice of my friend Tanja A., my former high-school friend, college friend, and room-mate at our landlord's apartment in Gajeva Street in Zagreb. She came home from Slovenia for the summer. She wanted us to meet up. After four years of silence. For us go somewhere for a swim together. After four years of silence. Her not calling me. Her not asking what happened to my child, is she alive, is she well, has she survived the horrors. I refused. The conversation was short and ended with my quick: "All right Tanja, bye!" I couldn't say it any other way.

By the way, I think the boy who disappeared in the "meat" smoke in Technical High School last Christmas was actually a nephew of hers. I remember him from when he was a little boy. He had a name. Indicative. Neven.[52]

3 April 1996

Nikša Antonini, my friend, was killed in a plane crash near Konavle.

Easter Day 1996

This past holiday was probably the saddest Easter celebrated in our home. Even though, after five depressing years of war, we should probably have especially looked forward to it.

The planned pint of best Belgian beer remains intact...

The newspaper photo of the plane broken in half in the hills above Konavle cannot be described with words. Photographers have an advantage: when confronted with a tragedy, they don't have to try to find – words.

Nikša's casual: "How are you doing down there?" – coming out of the phone during the war – takes on a whole new and unexpected meaning...

9 April 1996

If only I could grasp and take on at least part of Tina's pain![53]

Is there some kind of surgical procedure that could enable that?

17 April 1996

Promotion of *Pogledi* (*Views*) at the Society of Croatian Writers' Association in Zagreb.

The presenters were Petar Marija Radelj – Dominican friar, Ante Stamać – president of the Society, critic Božidar Petrač and dramatist

---

[52] In Croatian meaning "never fading"

[53] Tina was Nikša's wife and my friend.

Zlatko Crnković. Pavle (Paul) was also there. *To my closest – Peter and Paul – this means something. Is there some other saint on my side?*

30 April 1996

April is the cruellest month, breeding
Lilacs out of the dead land, mixing
Memory and desire - - -[54]

3 August 1996

Silvana left. Of her own free will. At 44 years of age. My conversations with her about the uselessness of her marriage have become useless. My gullet is excreting a metal taste into my mouth. *Even today, after so many years, in my mind I can hear her laughter ringing from her beautiful full lips.*

29 August 1996

(excerpt from the theatre review published in *Vijenac*)

- - - In their first press conferences, the organizers of the Zadar Theatrical Summer claimed that the biggest event of the project would be Goldoni's *The Cafeteria*. Today they claim it's *Poetic Doom*. Confusing. The inconsistencies of this story (which some might think irrelevant formalities) still lead us to the conclusion that it would be nice if two and two equalled – five. All in all, Zadar Theatre Summers offer a lot to Zadar and its citizens. Or, as the CEO of the Croatian Theatre House in Zadar said: "Zadar has recognized the theatre, the theatre has recognized Zadar." And that is much more important than individual profit. Even if individuals take the liberty and power to promote their own projects through the CTH, it remains unclear why one must wait, for example, until the congress of Croatian physicians at the end of September, or rather the beginning of autumn, to have an open air "summer" theatre premiere in relatively cold weather.

Maybe even the seasons have become the subjects of manipulation by privileged persons? All we can do is wait for the autumn to get some answers… Once again, the motto of this year's Theatre Summer: "Honesty and honour are of the highest importance to a man. And twice so to Zadar!"—

21 September 1996

I slowly enter St Anastasia's. It is big and empty. It's pleasant to surround oneself with solitude, quiet and invisible floating souls within the

[54] From *The Waste Land* by T. S. Eliot

cathedral. And even to succumb to the nostalgia of our dear ones, who are now gone.

15 October 1996

There's something special in the scents of the first half of October, when the nostrils widen with the sharp minty air between two showers in a sunny circle no warmer than the shade. The scent draws from the memory the souls of those who point to that which can but does not have to be.

3 January 1997

Year of the Woman (an unpublished article)

Some thirty years ago, American writer and poet Sylvia Plath wrote the following in her autobiographical novel *The Bell Jar*:

"I remembered Buddy Willard saying in a sinister, knowing way that after I had children I would feel differently, I wouldn't want to write poems any more. So I began to think maybe it was true that when you are married and have children it is like being brainwashed, and afterwards you go about as numb as a slave in a totalitarian state..."

Shortly after publishing this novel, Sylvia stopped writing poems. She was married, she was a mother, but her God-knows-which suicide attempt finally succeeded.

After this bleak introduction, I will point out that this is not an article on feminism (which I personally dislike because I believe that in itself it is a confirmation of two-way discrimination, and also because it's a term used with contempt as a label by men who have no "better argument" in a disagreement); this article is about women who desperately try to write poems/sing songs.

* * *

I will need two stories to serve as an example. First story: When Annie Mae Bullock, better known as Tina Turner, cut all ties to her addicted/dependant life of meek companion to her husband Ike, many people thought that the so-called weaker (meaning worse) half of the Ike & Tina couple was lost forever in the labyrinth of anonymity. Today, in her sixth decade of life, the "tigress", as they call her, enjoys the liberties of a life outside the marital and creative mould, performing concerts for entire stadiums of fans.

Second story: another "tigress" threw a bouquet of roses into her manager's face during an argument at a reception. When the enraged manager threw a glass of champagne into her face, she poured her own glass of champagne on her head, thus showing that no one can do anything to her which she herself cannot do as well. The singer in question was Bette Midler, and the reception was held for the premiere of the cult movie *Rose*, in which Bette portraits Rose, a singing star who is unable to confront her aggressive and manipulative manager. But, Bette is obviously not Rose...

Tina and Bette are no poets in the conventional sense, but they represent great names of the rock/pop scene in which (female) singers are not just the simple interpreters of music and lyrics written by someone else, they offer their own texts and therewith their own personality. For the past twenty years, next to Tina and Betty stood/stand other "tigresses" such as Debbie Harry – Blondie, Chrissie Hynde, Cyndi Lauper, Madonna... This ever greater influence of women on the scene can perhaps be connected to the flood of styles and rhythms that mark this specific period. They say that the first and the last followers of every fashion are ridiculous. If we focus on 80s music and apply this phrase to the rock and pop music of that particular decade, we might conclude that the styles, faces and trends were changing at such a fast pace that you never knew who would turn out to be ridiculous. Despite the rather obvious economic stagnation and growing number of young unemployed people, the 80s were a time when the wishes of youth, as well as their easy-going joy and flame didn't fade away. On the contrary, it seems as if the breakdown of the economy proved to be fertile ground for an even more fiery greed for musical pleasure. This inspired one music critic to compare the youth of the 80s to the band that played for the dancing passengers on the sinking Titanic.

It was a time of musical variety: anthological sighs of the enraptured and (voyeuristic) captivating subordination to the partner of Jane Birkin, the French singer whose song "*Je t'aime*" sounds so – French, romantic and even "innocent" in comparison to the orgasmic, electronic mix of sighs and metronomic disco rhythm of Donna Summer and other "computerized" performers of the 80s who often boiled down to an ironic document about female sexuality. Or even more hazardous: sexual self-sufficiency.

The messages of these vamps of the 80s rock/pop scene were based mostly on sexuality and aggressiveness – things that were previously forbidden fruit for the gender marked by masochism and self-sacrifice. The sweet innocence of Olivia Newton John, the female harmlessness of the breezy Kate Bush or the elegance of the singing Nefertiti – Sade Adu, remain significant, but the qualities of their expression will not attract whole stadiums of people as will the "tigresses" from the beginning of the article. Besides, even in literature, "chaste" characters do not have the potential to become heroes. They are too neutral, even too boring to become "legends".

Resisting averageness, subordination and the usual preconceptions of a woman sinner/sufferer – the new Joans of Arc of the rock art save their Land of Honesty even though they eventually end up on the stake of eros, anger and vengeance. The extreme sensuality of female extrovert introverts (or vice versa) is no easy-going quality because it provokes the spite and animosity of the "stronger" sex. A woman offering emotions and her "heart on a plate" – sometimes understood as a sort of prostitution – often encounters the madding indifference of men who feel more comfortable with an ulcer than with tears and confessions. HE, used to a cooked meal and fresh laundry, does not want to enter the complicated mechanism that is a woman's feelings under any circumstances. At least not when his own woman is in question.

Concerning this not especially appealing side of a woman's sensitivity, British singer Alison Moyet once said that she liked the singing style of black singers because they were ready to express those less lovely characteristics of women: possessiveness, jealousy and unscrupulousness. Alison's song *All Cried Out* is a true anthem to breaking up with female addictiveness and shallow subordination which offers a mirage of non-loneliness because the man is physically (but *only* physically) present.

However, the aforementioned forbidden fruit of free expression is not easy to obtain. In order to express all those hidden and suppressed taboo messages, singers often use various means that will make them equal or at least bring them closer to men, even if only seemingly. Some singers, like Annie Lenox or Sinead O'Connor, take on an androgynous image of a woman who seems to "depersonalize man who depersonalizes woman"... Others, who don't agree with an image of a bisexual with short "brushy" hair, wearing men's suits and with flattened breasts, remain feminine in their appearance but only because they have been blessed with a "profitable" coarse voice like that of Rod Stewart. Such raw sensuality can be heard in the voices of Elkie Brooks, Bonnie Tyler, Joan Armatrading and the great singer and movie star Cher.

There is also a type of singer who is not blessed with an appearance of special appeal, and therefore nurtures an image of a carefree and somewhat messy witch who always has something to say. Passionate Italian singer Gianna Nannini, best known in our parts for her performances of the World Cup soccer anthem, can afford the look of a street vendor from Ponterosso because she has such an enormous musical talent. Nannini seems mannish during her performances, and she summarizes her arrogance in one of her songs by saying to her lover: "Chi sa chi vincerà?" (Who knows who will win?) Despite her energetic and unfeminine style, Gianna Nannini has fan clubs all over western Europe.

The fourth type of female singer chooses to wear a lot of lipstick, a smile showing their pearly teeth and, naturally, bleached hair the colour of a faded dandelion – the look of a century-old archetype embodied in Marilyn Monroe, which was rediscovered in the form of Debbie Harry, Kim Wilde, Anna Oxa, Annie Lennox and finally megastar Madonna, who is described in Mike Clifford's rock encyclopaedia beginning with the sentence: "Sometimes, image is bigger than music." In these parts, this type was embodied first in the now forgotten "computerized" Marina Perazić, Zadar's Eurovision Taichee, Vanna with her extraordinary voice and the much more coquettish, platinum-blonde version in the form of Kasandra. Nevertheless, it seems today that a carefully constructed image requires an extraordinary amount of talent to back it up.

When considering this boom of female affirmation in rock music and refuting the usual belief about women in rock music being just second rate performers – the question that comes to mind is how do our own "tigresses", who, it seems, really do exist, function. Beside the extraordinary but never commercialized voices of Josipa Lisac and Zorica Kondža, in the past years, we see new voices, the provocative, dark-haired and natural I Bee with her "woods" and "givings", and also Alka, who is ready to "lie".

The ever more obvious stress on the cradle, the family as the nucleus of society and other Illyrian romantic models, other than that they have become obsolete over time, seem more and more paradoxical from our perspective. Maybe a sentimental American lifestyle allows such models because they are foremost based on high standards and other preconditions, which are not attached to the anxiety and uncertainty that go together with our current political and social changes. The (for the nth time) awakening of the nation combined with the constant threat of war is faced, unfortunately, with the massive frustration of both the female and male parts of society, with the inexorably rising number of people living on welfare, people with a bottle in their pocket, number of beaten-up women and neglected children. Our almighty *pater familias* ever more perceives his role as the family provider as a mistake. In the same fight for who will bring the bread to the table, a woman, despite the return to classic conceptions, has no privileges. In fact, seemingly emancipated, a woman is still expected to provide, unlike the so-called non-emancipated fat American wife and mother who buys hamburgers and pizzas for her children's lunch.

I remember the lyrics of Chrissie Hynde: “She wants to be a good mother/So she’ll do the best she can/ But what about the other?/What about the man?”

Considering the circumstances, I dare predict that our everyday man will not be looking for an angry, aggressive and butch woman creature on the stage. He will probably seek an apparition of a woman who is not desecrated by daily life. He will need a Botticellian beauty, covered in pastel, virgin veils, who bears no connection to bankruptcies, companies and inter-ethnic conflict. Besides, why would he look for a tigress or a witch on the stage when he already has one back home?

However, maybe women should make some kind of a bargain with their men. If we remember Sylvia Plath from the beginning of this text, we could expect the “weaker” sex to shout: ALLOW US TO KEEP WRITING OUR SONGS!

À propos of songs, can they be illustrated with the following lyrics?

(Kasandra:) If the night were ten times as long/ It would still be too little time with me...

(Alka:) You ride like Johnny Wayne/ Tonight the whole world is yours...

(I Bee:) Swim-ming-at-night, I’ll nibble the salt from your skin...

Speaking of salt, I suppose that no one will be able to say that relations between the sexes are – insipid!

5 January 1997

For a considerable number of Zadar’s citizens 1997 began with the “New Year’s Ball” (or so it was announced!) – a mix of socio-realistic predictability and the unscrupulousness of the first pillar of capitalism, in the ballroom of Hotel Novi Park. It was one of the first celebrations at that hotel after the war; until recently it was occupied by refugees. After paying a good sum money *per capita* for something that occurs once a year, we – lightly dressed in festive clothes – were welcomed by a uninspected (meaning a table behind a pillar!) room without heating, the surround system was dead after some minute and a half of the band’s performance, the dancers were falling all over the dance floor, which was slippery because of the leaking roof, the waiters – confused by the stampede of guests and being accustomed to refugee customs – served us expensive wine in the same glasses that this hotel uses as toothbrush holders…. This was a confirmation of the high quality and preparedness of this “end” of the world for the upcoming tourist season.

8 January 1997

Dear Uncle Vlasto[55],

You will probably be surprised by this letter. I have started to write it so many times (I even finished some of them in my own mind).

I don't even remember when we last saw each other. There is such a gulf of time between us that it is very hard for me to write. Since I last saw you a lot has happened that has drawn me away – in a real battle for bare survival – from many of my (previous) contacts. The period from 1991 up until now has turned into a sort of a mess and it is difficult to point out individual events and evaluate them separately.

In the autumn of 1991, the war began, and with it probably the most difficult time in my life (provided I don't live to see another war!). My daughter Ema was a year and 7 months old when the shootings and bombings began. A lot of people were killed in the city alone, even among civilians, and the hardest part of it all was living with the thought that at any moment there was a pretty good chance that something terrible might happen to my child.

In the autumn of 1992, S. and I split up and divorced at my request (we were separated for a while and our divorce was the logical consequence of everything that preceded it). The war, the divorce, a small child, shortage of water, electricity, food... I need go no further – it was horrible, but I hope now it's over. Although, there are some new problems arising right now: if war can be shown as something black, than the post-war period is definitely soaked in grey.

The fact that I know nothing of how you live your life confuses me. Whenever I think of you, I dwell on how bizarre it is that we are not in touch and that we don't see each other in these hard times. I've asked my dad occasionally if he knew how you were doing, but he usually gave me some very vague answers.

Have you thought about visiting us for a while?

I must admit that I see or hear from Mum and Dad rarely. In the past few years (I guess due to the war, the divorce, different views on family relations and other matters) we have become somehow estranged. Or maybe that family closeness that Dad was trying to maintain was in fact an

[55] The letter is addressed to my father's cousin, Vlastimir (Vlasto) Peričić, professor of composition at the Belgrade Music Academy. His father Jure, my grandfather's brother, went to study history and geography to Belgrade (at the time, Zagreb did not offer those subjects). He married a professor of (at that time called) the "Serbo-Croat" language, Jelica (I was supposed to be named Jelena, after her), and he never returned to Croatia. This letter is also the only letter in the past ten years that I have sent to Serbia.

illusion when it came to important things. It is hard, and even too hard to bear the exclusiveness and patriarchal views within our family and therefore I have come to the conclusion that it is a great spiritual crime to enable education and intellectual progress to someone only to force him/her, even when one turns 35 years of age, to live inside "Mediterranean pigeon-holes" where male/female relationships take on monstrous proportions. But, I don't want to bother you with such matters any longer.

I would really like to know how you're doing, how your health is and whether you need anything.[56] This time gap between us, as I said, has been too long. But I believe that it is not unsurpassable. Get in touch.

Love and best wishes.

Helena

21 January 1997

The only venue in Zadar that brings me back my faith in being informed and discipline is the Scientific Library, with its composure and order. It received the City of Zadar Award in 1995 for maintaining a high quality of work even during the war and after the war. And well deserved. I glance at the students occupied with their books inside the sunny reading room. Spiritual curiosity, openness towards new ideas, together with an enormous amount of tolerance, high-spiritedness, altruism... – is the essence of intellectuality blooming in such places?

23 January 1997

Defence of my doctoral thesis at the Faculty of Philosophy in Zadar. The grading committee included Dr. Košutić-Brozović, Dr. Beker and Dr. Mardešić. I last saw Dr. Professor Beker, my former mentor, during my postgraduate studies. He travelled back to Zagreb after lunch. Melancholic question: will it be another ten years till we meet again?

My PhD thesis "Mediators of English Literature in Croatian Literary Critique Between 1914 and 1940" was based on the research of bibliographies of critiques, translations and theatrical repertoires from that period, which I conducted by myself. The central part of this dissertation

---

[56] At the time of revising the fragments of these entries for publication in a Zagreb journal, Belgrade, where uncle Vlasto lived, was nicknamed Bombay. Vlastimir Peričić was a composer, artist, astrologist, polyglot, first-rate intellectual (Vienna Conservatory), humanist, scholar, pacifist... At the time, he lived on the top floor of a building in Vasina, in the city centre. By that time he was already a total invalid and confined to a wheelchair. What he would not, however, forgo under any circumstance were – cigarettes...

about the reception of English literature consists of ten monographs about the most distinguished figures of literary criticism. Torbarina, Horvat, Krišković, Maraković and others... I am glad I brought to light some of the names which have been previously marginalized or completely pushed back. Although, it seems to me that the results of my six-year work, some during the war some not, sound like frogs croaking in a pond? Are we really at the back of beyond I am sometimes shaken up in that belief by some event such as the Zadar hackers breaking into the computer security system of the US military? Is the Pentagon nearer than the neon-lit book shops near Jelačić Square?

Mediators. I think we should be aware of the role of mediators (critics, translators, theatre directors) as well as the reader himself in the reception of literature. Actually, the entire algorithm of postmodernist literary procedure is based on the consciousness of the reader's "writing of the text by reading". Intertextuality, alterity, ironizing, simultaneousness... – all spring from the perspective of the imaginary reader. The author is the one who textually forms conceptions which he gets by simulating the perspective of the recipient, the recipient's conscience. Sometimes I consciously trivialize my own emotion and literary act on paper. Not because I think I am superior to this act. On the contrary: I fear it. Just like I fear the reader. Why? The reader is superior because he carries the burden of multiple choices. He has the Internet. He owns the world. And all I have is words. And this street in Voštarnica. Poorly lit.

25 January 1997

Hall of the Faculty of Philosophy. Professor S. O., one of the heads of the Zadar branch of the Croatian Heritage Foundation stops me and reminds me of our agreement regarding the collection of the Student Literary Club, which I have been leading since its foundation in 1994. He expects me to choose the texts for the book they intend to publish and to write an introduction. One can hardly imagine what kind of work this is: to decipher ten different poetic worlds. I had prepared a book of works by the Club members ready for publication back in 1994, the works of ten young men and women, but no one (not even the Faculty they study at) showed any kind of interest in publishing this 70-page-long booklet. Maybe we'll have more luck this time. The kids are ambitious, and what's more important: a great many of them are talented. We will still hear about them in the future.

27 January 1997

Last weekend, a "Zadar convoy" headed for Rome, consisting of four buses with the representatives of the Faculty of Philosophy in Zadar, of the archbishopric and Zadar City Hall. Thus, the celebration of the great Zadar anniversaries – 600 years since the foundation of the first Croatian university within the Dominican convent and 400 years of the Faculty of Philosophy – "got its epilogue" (*Narodni List*). For this occasion, they presented the Pope with a monograph written by Krasić on Zadar's Open University. Many people ask me what's going on with the renewed Zadar University that has been talked about for the past ten years. Would it be a betrayal of local patriotic feelings if I were to answer them by saying: Can one build a university in a city where the tenants of the only students' hall of residence live without any heating or hot water, where there is no decent cinema (the only one bears the name *Victory*?!), where there have been only two plays featured at the theatre since the beginning of the season, where there is no Student Club, where young people meet either in brass-furnished cafes or at the former City Cafe furbished with rubbish presented as a "postmodern interior"? Or on street corners where they ask people for change to buy themselves another joint. Gentlemen, offer them something in exchange for New Zealand!

2 February 1997

Ema's seventh birthday. Baking cakes need to be "squeezed" in somewhere between World Literature exams, ironing piles of clothes, writing requested texts... Above the stove a favourite sign of mine says: "Make lunch – not war!"

3 February 1997

Carnival – a special story. For the past few years, for each carnival Zadar organizes a real – "carnival". They ask for money from business sponsors, from the City and County administrations to organize a joyous folk festivity with penis-like and breast-like rubber masks. The only thing lacking to make a full impression at the Roman Forum is Caligula himself. Nevertheless, one could say that such atavistic events are just "what the people ordered". Let us have some fun at least for a day (or night)! Let us make monkeys out of ourselves when everyone else is making us into monkeys the rest of the year! Of course, there are always those who make a pretty penny out of the whole situation. Last year, the author of the texts for the carnival mayor and governor (Go freelance artists!) received more than 5000 kunas. For a few pages of text. Respect! One must know how to grab the opportunity. When there is one. I salute you, author! And you, author, take off your mask!

17 February 1997

I went to Šibenik to make some introductory comments at the presentation of the freshly printed *Vila Dalmatinska* by Zorčić, first published in Zadar 145 years ago. Naturally, the reprint was published by the industrious Šibenik Juraj Šižgorić City Library. Their staff – Milivoj, Saša[57], Vili etc. are embarrassed to hear compliments for their own work. "Spare us that rhetorical kitsch!" they tell me. My God, do people even know how much effort is needed to publish books in such places as Zadar and Šibenik? *The Tale of Two Cities* doesn't end with the last shell in the Homeland War; it continues, unfortunately, through an economy that was thrown to its knees, through lowered artistic and creative standards, through supposedly "birth-of-the-state" poetry evenings, when the use of the aorist and imperfect are considered stylistic peaks, through the shameless glorifying and demanding of patriotism from podiums in front of which the handless, legless or blind sit in the first row. Do you know what it means to publish a book in such a milieu? I remember the beginnings and the initiation of *Glasje* back in 1992. We knocked in vain on all the right doors seeking a sponsor's charity to print the journal while the shells were whistling above our heads. I remember the preparation for my scenic collage *Colleague, the War Is Going on for Too Long...* inside the shabby building of the Puppet Theatre, which we were allowed to use as a faculty drama group. At that time, May 1995, Zagreb was attacked. Luka, a little boy from Zadar, was injured then. Books, plays, radio shows – feverish childish hope for mental and spiritual survival. In those binary times when all that mattered was if you're there or not. Can one really measure the difficulty of such work, which wasn't actually considered work but existential need?

19 February 1997

Morning coffee at the Branimir cafe with my namesake Helena Roguljić, the only woman member of the Zadar affiliation of DHK[58]. Another one of her books of poetry is being published soon. Accidentally, we both chose the same Zadar printing house, with a symptomatic name –

[57] Just ten days after this dinner, Saša M., a talented and hard-working young cherisher of the literary word departed for Canada (without notifying most of his friends and acquaintances). He will probably never return here. At least not as a Croatian citizen.
[58] Croatian Writers' Association

GAFF. *Nomen est omen.* The printing of my collection *Views... (Something Like... Intrusive Entries)* took over a year and a half with those printers. Helena's book was supposed to have been published over two months ago. The "professionalism" of the owner of the printing house became obvious with the (author's) humiliating phone calls and (the printer's) promises ending with a "Soon...". I suppose this "soon" in many cases turns into "posthumous"... The two of us comment on last year's General Meeting of the Zadar branch of DHK and their choice of some fifty people of letters (or money!) as their associate members. A farce. A cover up for those who know how to use the situation. Zadar is becoming a Mecca for showbiz literary/commercial inspirations. Cheers!

21 February 1997

I'm leafing through *Narodni List*, which is still pulling it off without a proof-reader. (The oldest newspaper in the Balkans will start sounding like Istrian-Kvarner papers. With leaking grammar and spelling.) Within the same edition, two interviews with common ground: Zadar Croatian Theatre House (HKK). An interview with the acting director of the HKK, Vera Stipčević (also the director of the Zadar Puppet Theatre) and an interview with the Zadar and (half-)Pag county head Prtenjača. Too many suspicious things have been happening with our theatre in the past year.

23 February 1997

I found out that the Concert Office in Zadar is preparing a performance of the Zadar Chamber Orchestra and soloists from abroad. Each such announcement causes remorse: whenever I meet Mrs. Branka D. in town, the enterprising director of the Concert Office, especially sentimental towards wartime subscribers, I have to apologize to her for not attending the concerts anymore. They stopped using the theatre hall as their venue because the Office became independent of the HKK. How can I explain to Branka that their concerts no longer present an "escape from life"? They hold their performances in the same place where I go to work – at the Faculty of Philosophy. Besides, I don't dance when/where others are playing. Which further complicates matters, obviously.

24 February 1997

I missed the premiere of the new play at the Puppet Theatre entitled *Dream of the Wandering Actor* or *The Princess and the Pea* because of Zorčić. Until further notice, the play will be performed on Sundays, in the old building naturally, in Jazine. The director of the play is Bulgarian, known by the pseudonym Sunny Sunninsky. This is his fourth performance with the Zadar puppeteers since last summer. The only actor in the play is Zlatko Košta, who has won an award as Croatia's best puppeteer. The play is actually a recognition of Zlatko. In Zadar, people are masters of puppeteering. So much so in fact that second place at national and international competitions is considered a failure. Many more premieres will have to pass until the new puppet theatre building is finished. They announced Carić's adaptation of *The Mountains* for this summer. I'm afraid that this project will also end as most of their other "difficult" plays. Why don't they at least perform puppet shows more often? These plays could even be performed in the squares.

When you place talent between poverty and megalomania – what do you get? A Zadar sandwich of frustration and dejection.

28 February 1997

The smell of spring. The smell of the election. What will become of Zadar this year? Will the City and the County administrations stop "biting" each other and find some mutual understanding? And will *Jedan u kope – drugi u špade*[59] stop being the underlying principle of functioning of the (non)culture of the north Dalmatian Babylon? I heard that another telephone is thrown away almost every day at the offices of Zadar City Hall. And that something is usually broken as well: like a crystal ashtray or a vase. In a town ruled by cholerics, one should find some room for culture.

I hear that some people from the City and the County administrations never read the papers. And that they don't like doing errands away from the Zadar Peninsula (where they usually live and work). Could one dub it a phobia? And the Peninsula is enclosed within the city walls. It's a place where people from the islands are the bosses. Who plant their island Robinson Crusoe mentality into the City's way of life – self-sufficient, self-satisfied. How can a person – who rushes back to his island during the weekend, to his olives – spread cultural insights and create better conditions for typically "weekend" institutions – such as the cinema, theatre, museums.

I dream of flying into the world. I notice that even my World Literature class is considered by some a subject not compatible with the turbo-nationalistic spirit. But tell me please, how can I teach Držić without mentioning Plautus and the Italian Renaissance?

Maybe we'll go to Spain just before the summer: Cristina and Judith have been inviting us for years. They were two of the few (meaning those

[59] Literal translation "One plays in coppe, the other in spades", referring to suits in Italian cards called Carte Triestine and meaning that the two players cannot agree on something

that can be counted on the fingers of one hand) who offered in panic while the war was raging to take Ema in. Maybe it's people like them that make it all worth while. The war was a burden for everyone. (Except for the profiteers.) And maybe it makes no sense to talk about it with the people who haven't felt it in the way that it makes you into a person full of spite. The war was a tremendous waste of time; it brought with it too much foolishness to be able to make peace with the load of absurdities happening right now. If I say to someone in Zagreb that a young country is a child, but a child that needs to be brought up because children are goods that go bad easily, that person usually gives me a look and almost always says in anger (never even knowing how offensive what they are saying is) that they are "a true patriot". I don't know, maybe the provincial patriotism of those of us situated under Velebit should be measured by some ruler from Mars. Besides, talking about wartime experiences to those who haven't even touched its pulse means causing unease in the listener. It's the same as talking about bowel problems to nice people.

1 March 1997

Blessed February: it is so short. My assistant's pay cheque is knocking at the door.

The World. And the Peninsula/Island.[60]

People in Zagreb call Zadar "the sea" or ... "blooming almonds". And what should I call it? "The-place-where-I-receive-letters-from-the-world".

17 July 1997

Parading or Parodying? (*Narodni List*)

"Oh beautiful, oh beloved, oh sweet freedom..." – the words from Gundulić's work *Dubravka* recited by a handsome actor, a guest from Zagreb, one hot night in July in front of a white baldachin stretched by a group of young men and women above their heads...

Such an image will surely remind us of the opening of the Dubrovnik Summer Festival, a festivity that celebrates the power and freedom of the white fortified city on the Adriatic. But this image reappeared a few nights ago, however, this time not in Dubrovnik but in Zadar; on Monday, on the National Square during the grand opening of the first Zadar Theatrical Summer. Various things were mixed up in the scenario of this event. Let us mention some of the moments without following a specific chronological order.

The festivity began with a performance by a contemporary dance

---

[60] At some points in Zadar's history, the Peninsula was turned into an island by digging a moat on its landward side.

ensemble, based on a musical piece that reminds one simultaneously of a gypsy choir and Vangelis's endless synthesizer compositions. A stylistic musical switch occurred when the Zadar madrigalists (naturally, dressed in Renaissance costumes) sang the national anthem *Lijepa Naša* (*Our Beautiful*). Then the aforementioned actor from Zagreb read out loud some kind of an introductory note trying very hard with great difficulty to read the handwriting, only to invite another guest actor (who most definitely had either had a few drops to drink or smoked a joint). For some time, the two of them kept arguing so one couldn't tell if the announced actors – who, as the two warned us, were to play in this summer's Zadar comedies – would show up in the spotlight or not. Then the Zadar-Knin "governor", as he was announced by the handsome moderator, paid tribute to the spiritual sufferings of Zadar's citizens who didn't lose their desire for theatre even in wartime (especially if one has in mind that in our town, the habit of visiting theatrical plays usually doesn't go beyond the premieres!). The festivity moderator tried once again to read from his papers and even though he had a strong voice, the poor thing would even stutter once in a while, thus ensuring a somewhat grotesque effect.

While he was trying so hard, behind him drove by a group of garbage men on their small garbage truck, welcomed with enthusiastic applause from the audience. Individual scenes kept changing in a neat disorder with the worthy quotes from Zadar and Croatian cultural heritage: Baraković, Zoranić, Preradović and some Milutin Cihlar Nehajev. All of that, neatly cut out, mixed up and fixed up was spiced up with a strange intrusive lack of good taste (which at moments took on blasphemous proportions), based primarily on the fact that the guest actor, the programme moderator, who, I presume, would receive a fee, saw his lines for the first time at exactly 10 pm, under the stage lights.

If by some chance the guest from Zagreb – who I'm sure can play brilliant roles when they make *sense* – had to read that accursed text at the opening of the Summer Festival in Dubrovnik, maybe the honoured professional actor would have dedicated more of his professional attention to the text he was given (because everyone knows what Dubrovnik is: a place where Hamlet has been played by Derek Jacobi, Daniel Day Lewis and the like), but it seems that some believe that, for a Zadar audience, even this miserable improvisation was – milk and honey. The unprepared and clumsy direction, or, better put, (someone's personal) arrangement of the entire grand opening of the Zadar Theatre Summer turned into pure insolence towards those who perceived the garbage truck drive-through "stunt" behind the stage as the only spontaneous and inspiring moment of the entire "spectacle" – luckily, there were two (2) such moments, a "return ticket"! I believe that even those authentic moments that caused such enthusiasm in the audience were well sponsored.

A Zadar audience is used to being sold a bill of goods wrapped in theatrical cellophane once in a while – they don't expect more than that. And this is the attitude of the curators of souls from our Theatre House. Or maybe the most important thing is that "something is happening" in this town? I am convinced that it would be better if nothing was happening than such "somethings": cheap (maybe even profitable for some) festivities toned with imperative patriotism are not polite things to burden on an ordinary man with a war on his back. If some have a strong desire to make the Zadar Theatrical Summer into a tradition, it would be wonderful if they wouldn't turn such "triumphant" grand openings into a habit.

If it's true that some Zadar theatre people well known to us were involved in the preparations of this curiosity that consists of misused lyrics "Dawn has broken – Day will come" – not as critics but as spectators – then I must ask honestly: Was this really necessary?

And so, fifty years after the foundation of the Zadar Croatian National Theatre (a fact mentioned on the posters announcing the Theatrical Summer), dawn has broken, but apparently for someone who misused it for drunken parading and parodying of the Dubrovnik Summer Festival at the main Zadar square (no less).

Dawn has broken.[61] What about the day?

13 September 1997

My life closed twice before its close;
It yet remains to see
If Immortality unveil
A third event to me—[62]

Dream

Midway upon the journey of our life...[63] At the age of thirty five... I stand on the top of the hill. Amongst the clouds and the wind. They appear from the bottom of the hill, one by one. Their steps are slow, almost floating, suppressing gravity and other laws of physics. Not even the strong south wind disturbs them. I fear they will turn around and leave. But they keep approaching, never pausing, never hesitating; airy, with pale faces and watery eyes with distinctively red rims around their eyelids. Like

---

[61] Allusion to a verse by Petar Preradović, Croatian poet (1818-1872)
[62] From a poem by the American poet Emily Dickinson
[63] The opening verse of Dante's *Inferno*

old people's. I don't know who they really are (it's hard to recognize them from a great distance). Wind and raindrops – scarce but big and heavy – whipped their faces: their hair was fluttering, their moist clothes stuck to their bodies.

I was first approached by Niko. He looks the freshest of them. Probably because he was the last to join them. His face shows the best.

With large long-sighted lenses in gilded metal frames, he was jumping around – with his belly – up and down, cheerful as always. He was carrying a small barrel of the best Belgian beer (which we never got to taste) under one of his arms. A bundle of photographs under the other arm. He approached me overjoyed, and then looked me straight in the eyes. At that moment, the smile vanished from his face, the barrel went downhill and the photographs were scattered around by the wind. They were mostly black and white. He believes that colour takes away the dignity from photographs: that it is affected in situations when every affectation actually means blasphemy. They were snapshots from rock concerts, political meetings, photographs of flowers, crosses, guns, mothers wearing headscarves, children with twisted faces. The only colour photo was the one depicting his wife and daughter; they are unusually alike – with long eyelashes on regularly shaped green-brown eyes, like the fruits of the sweet Dalmatian plant jujube.

Niko was followed by a column formed by: Snježana's brother, an unquestionable talent for mathematics and physics, then Lada's sister, then little Luka, who should have become a great movie director, Chester Beers – Vietnam veteran and poet, then Tanja's seventeen-year-old nephew Neven, then a young man – a son of one of my colleagues – who stuck his head out of the window of a moving tram one drunken night, then the brother of a colleague from Philosophy who was shot one night in his Croatian army uniform in some cafe in Split, the blinded boy from Srebrenica, the girl Irma from Sarajevo, then the soldiers from Sukošan, most of them of the same age as my brother, who were killed near Škabrnja... Those who were dear to me, and those I barely knew, or those whom I've read about in the papers but were close to people I worked with, hung out with, was friends with... – I recognized them all, even though I don't know the names of some of them. And they're all hopping like ballerinas, with cheerful faces, scarless, spared of the consequences of someone else's or their own violence over their bodies. When they all finally approached me, they put the things they were carrying on the ground – blind man's canes, guns, logarithmic tables, cameras, medicines, bombs – they took each others hands and surrounded me, like in a wheel dance, laughing, dancing, giggling, stepping in and out of the clouds and winds... *Danse macabre – danse macabre – danse ma-ca-bre…* The wind blew relentlessly. It was getting dark and the night was cut repeatedly by flashes of lightning. The earth was getting wet and I felt each clump jumping on the ground under the force of the huge raindrops. I wondered: what is it like for you under the ground, what is it like on this windy and rainy night, how do you bear the weight of this sky on your laid-out bodies.

17 November 1997

Dear Petar[64],

I assume you'll be surprised by this letter because I haven't written to you in a long time and you probably thought I would never write to you again.

One of the reasons I haven't written – and I believe that you wouldn't accept it that way – is that writing letters to someone far away from this stale, killer, Marinkovićian[65] milieu makes no sense whatsoever. Any blabbering of the author of a letter about the misery – both spiritual and the type that is supposedly not important (said by those who have never experienced real material misery) – humiliates both the author of this letter and the one reading the letter.

Why then write to someone who is so far away from all this? Simply because: I feel speechless from the great distance to Switzerland (*Emily Dickinson…*[66]), from that (maybe ostensible but still felt) "purity" that surrounds you and which I dare to bite at with my miserable Slavic frustrations, my aggressive (pre)Balkan inferiority and millennia-long half-savagery.

This year flew by like a dream and it seems to me as though January and my thesis defence were only yesterday. The summer went "down the drain" in cleaning the garbage from the old house of Darko's grandfather in Petrčane, which has lain abandoned for at least a quarter of a century, which is damp, built on no real foundations, and full of rotting and unnecessary things that Darko's father piled up in it.

It's almost midnight and Ema is asleep next to me after a long day of conversations about her dad. Beside these minor and yet enormous emotional and existential problems of my 7.9-year-old daughter, I'm swamped in the quarrels within my own family (in my relationship with my parents, with my brother...) with the metal taste of anti-patriarchal

---

[64] Petar is the Croatian form for the name Peter. It refers to the same person as the entry on 17 April 1996.

[65] Allusion to Ranko Marinković

[66] Allusion to Dickinson's poem *Our Lives are Swiss*

quarrels of heightened tone, lost in advance, and quasi-intellectual, superficial and demeaning arguments.

Zagreb was and remains distant. In fact, it's getting more and more distant. There hasn't been any kind of play in Zadar for months, and a concert is held – and thank heavens if it is – once in a month and a half (and when it does occur, I don't go because they are usually held at the Faculty of Philosophy: I don't feel like going to concerts where I work).

It is not easy to decide to live here.

Ema has grown up into a beautiful girl with big eyes and a heart full of joy (or at least with a lot of desire for a heart full of joy). I give her as much love as I can, seeking the last atoms of energy of my scoliotic body destroyed by sitting, typing, thinking... Every night, I lie down next to her until she falls asleep. And that's the sweetest part of my day/night. To lie down next to that pure and enormous child's soul.

It would be wonderful if you would get in touch.

Best wishes.

Helena

17 January 1998

At the sitting of our Department, an older colleague linguist sat down opposite me at the table and scattered in front of me cut-out articles I wrote for *Vijenac* and my interview published in the New Year edition of *Zadarski List*. The colleague was obviously well prepared for this meeting and decided to talk seriously about my texts and statements concerning the status of my subject World Literature within the framework of Croatian Studies at the Zadar Faculty. Luckily, the meeting got prolonged and the colleague was forced to go somewhere else before he had the chance to speak. A few months ago, he approached me on the street (in front of St Simon's Church, even though he presents himself as a great Catholic!) and suggested that he (as a linguist!) and two other professors – a distinguished expert awaiting retirement with a sad face but cheerful heart, and a guest professor, dramatist with a whole array of regular monthly incomes (all of them experts in Croatian Studies – none of them a comparatist!) – form a Commission (sic!), which would set the programme and required reading list for my subject – World Literature.

***

We will never drink Bruderschaft
Nor relish
Polemics unrecorded by the media

Without the scientific apparatus, my colleague,
I conclude: I am not a man of bribes (mea culpa)
And I do not write in decasyllables (mea culpa)

And – neither you nor I have the time for
That small difference
Between idiocies and maxims

And I will not let you teach me
How to love Croatia
How to hate Croatia

(Because) the enduring have taught me how not to endure
By sitting in the last row
Of my own principles (cheap seats)—[67]

EPILOGUE (1999):

1. Brother of Snježana T. – he took his life by shooting himself in the head with his father's gun in September 1991 – at the beginning of all this.

2. The son of my colleague M. S. – killed in an accident while riding the tram in Zagreb in 1993.

3. Autumn of 1993 in Zadar – plenty of suicides.

4. Sister of Lada S. – took her life in spring 1994 by throwing herself from a building in Voštarnica.

5. Grandson of an ex-colonel of the Yugoslav National Army killed himself by setting off bombs he was carrying around his waist. It happened during lunch break in one of the classrooms of the Technical High School, in November 1994.

6. The son of my colleague V. S. – Luka, a talented student of direction at the Zagreb Academy, succumbed to his wounds received during the bombing of Zagreb in May 1995.

7. Stepdaughter and son-in-law (and son-in-law's brother) of Professor A. F. killed in a car crash in 1995; one of the girls who survived will probably never be able to walk on her own again.

8. My colleague T.G.H.'s twin-brother committed suicide on 2 February 1995 in Skopje.

9. Nikša Antonini, photo reporter and a friend, died on 3 April 1996 in a plane crash: an American military plane that was transporting the political and economical delegation of the USA from Tuzla to Dubrovnik

[67] From my poem *Colleague, the War Is Going on for Too Long...*

hit the hill Sv. Ivan near Konavle. Till this day, his wife has never received any damages.

10. Exactly four months after Nikša's death, on 3 August 1996, my cousin committed suicide by throwing herself from the sixth floor. She was 44 years old.

11. From the beginning of 1999 till mid July of the same year, a total of twenty-six (26) suicides were committed in Zadar area. Half of them were war veterans, volunteers of the Homeland War.

—The rain is falling... and it's autumn... and it's war ... and Croatia
And I don't feel like chewing over
The supplement of the local papers—[68]

* * *

I said: When all this is over, I definitely won't have any time for my own foolishness and other people's spitefulness.

And I said: To my closest – Peter and Paul – this means something. Is there any other saint on my side?

[68] Continuation of the previously started poem

18. srpnja 1991.

Na užganoj, ljetnoj prašini... Sve te smrti... *Odmak od sentimentalnosti potaknute ratom nije moguć: kad sam ovo počela pisati, nisam, kao ni bilo tko pored mene, razmišljala - literarno.*

26. kolovoza 1991.

Već je protekla godina dana otkako su započeli sukobi sa Srbima u Hrvatskoj. Početno barikadiranje glavnih prometnica u Lici preraslo je u zločine kakvi se ne pamte od Drugoga svjetskog rata. *Zlo i strah pred zlom moraju biti individualizirani. Rat utopljen u mnoštvu gubi na značenju.*

Sama sam u stanu s Emom. S. je u Šibeniku. Svaku večer pred san molim anđele da sačuvaju ovo dijete što sada tako spokojno spava uza me. *Zasigurno nema težeg i razornijeg iskustva od bdijenja nad sudbinom vlastita djeteta u drastičnim okolnostima rata i nasilja...*

27. kolovoza 1991.

Rat se nastavlja. Sunčano i tiho poslijepodne u opreci je s onim što se zbiva u mjestima nedaleko Zadra. Neprestano slušam vijesti na radiju i televiziji. (To sam izbjegavala činiti cijeloga ljeta da bih bila mirnija, no sada sam s Emom sama u stanu pa želim biti obaviještena o onom što se zbiva u okolici grada.) Na radiju: upute za slučaj zračnog napada na grad. S. sutra putuje u Zagreb. Razmišljam da i Ema i ja nekamo otputujemo. Možda na sjever, prema Rijeci. U Lovran, kod tete Ane? Je li to kukavičluk?

Sutra će nam voda biti opet isključena. (Kao uostalom svakoga drugog dana odnedavno.) Govore o iskapanju novih izvora pitke vode u samom gradu. A toliko toga valja oprati. I Emu treba kupati... Ta Ema je navršila tek godinu i šest mjeseci…

Možda će sutra proglasiti ratno stanje i uvođenje opće mobilizacije. Pitam se dokad će ovo trajati? A kad se i završi - jer kad-tad se mora završiti - još uvijek će trajati sukobi. Diplomacija i pregovori neće zaustaviti terorizam, eksplozije, iskapčanje izvora vode... Što će biti - poslije?

31. kolovoza 1991.

Današnjim danom završava rok za povlačenje vojske iz Hrvatske. Zato mnogi ovu subotu nazivaju "danom D". Nadam se da ćemo doživjeti i sutrašnji dan, i prekosutrašnji, i onaj nakon njega...

1. rujna 1991.

Prizori televizijskih vijesti: odsječene ruke, iskopane oči, izmrcvarena tijela mrtvih. Sve što napišem zvuči banalno u odnosu na zbilju.

Ovaj vikend provodimo u Sukošanu. Zrikavci kao i svakoga ljeta zriču u obližnjim čempresima i tamarisu. Kao i svakog ljeta, vruće je, pa u "hodnicima" pod pokrivačem tragam za ponekom zaostalom strujom svježine. Kao i svakog ljeta, komarci zuje, i čini se da postaju sve nemilosrdniji i otporniji. Ljetna matrica trenutnog življenja u sjevernoj Dalmaciji kulisa je atavističke, instinktivne potrebe za nadom i vjerom u nekakvog boga koji će nam sigurno, prije ili kasnije, donijeti spas!

5. rujna 1991.

Da se kojim slučajem pojavi neka nova Gertrude Stein, možda bi ona i moju generaciju, rođenu početkom šezdesetih, nazvala "izgubljenom". Danas smo Branka, Rade, njegov brat Branko i ja posjetili Snježanu, čiji se brat prije par dana (u ponedjeljak) ubio. Bilo mu je 28 godina. Bio je izuzetno darovit mladić, završio elektrotehnički fakultet, nedavno dobio posao u Zadru i ... revolverom. Očevim. Je li se radilo o usamljenosti, tuzi za izgubljenom ljubavi ili je u ovoj beznadnoj, ratnoj svakodnevnici njegov bistar i senzibilan um zamračila i čašu prelila posljednja u nizu slika surovosti koje nas okružuju?

13. rujna 1991.

Danas mi je rođendan. Jubilarni. *Happy birthday !*

Svi koje sam danas srela i s kojima sam razgovarala kao da su zatečeni vlastitim strahom. Dok sam bila u Znanstvenoj knjižnici - toj oazi tišine, spokoja i koncentriranog posvećivanja saznavanju - zabilježene su poruke na sekretarici: zvale su Tina - koja se s godišnjaka vratila u Zagreb (kako joj zavidim što je gore!); zvala je iz Zagreba i Ana - Emina kuma, i Branka B. Sve njih zanima što je s nama: imamo li vode, hrane... Zasad imamo svega, osim slobode kretanja, vedrine i smijeha. Anu sam poslije podne bezuspješno pokušavala dobiti u Leksikografskom zavodu. Telefonske linije sa Zagrebom preopterećene su. Stanje je u Zadru očajno.

Danas su na vijestima rekli da je u Vukovaru među ostalim ubijeno i jedno petogodišnje dijete. Strah me je, silno me je strah: noževa, klanja, vlastita straha... Kažu da su topovske cijevi usmjerene prema Zadru i da su avioni spremni za napad na grad - grad kamenit i širok, utopljen u babljem ljetu. Koliko je samo sunca u gradu ovih dana! Kako je i Sunce slabašno pred nastupajućim dimom zgarišta, pred ruševinama stoljetnih zidina, pred krvlju razlivenom po drevnim pločnicima...? Jesu li ove minute zadnje koje otkucavaju prividnim mirom ovoga kraja?

16. rujna 1991.

Subotnja "proslava" moga tridesetog rođendana bila je vrlo kratka (društvo se povuklo kući već oko devet navečer). Pozvala sam prijatelje misleći kako je dobro da se nađemo - možda s nekima i zadnji put - (*... što se pokazalo točnim!*) u ovim okolnostima. Iako su me neki podržali u nakani da upriličim druženje, znam da je većina nerado došla. Mislila sam da ću biti vedar domaćin koji neće dopustiti da se odviše razglaba o ratnim nedaćama. Uz kolačiće i par boca vina sve se doimalo prilično "normalnim". A onda je na teren vojarne udaljene tek tridesetak metara sletio helikopter. Neki su od nas otišli na balkon promatrati slijetanje. Iz okolice Zadra počele su odzvanjati eksplozije. No, kada je Marina P., čuvši prve detonacije - počela drhtati - taj je strah u meni izazvao isprva nelagodu i nesigurnost a potom moj vlastiti pravi strah, koji me je postupno paralizirao. Tako sam se prestala uključivati u razgovor i ništa mi više nije bilo dovoljno smiješno. (Iako je Rade, po svom običaju, pokušavao nabaciti par štoseva.) *Rade i sada živi s obitelji u Zadru. Marina i Nenad s djevojčicom žive negdje u Belgiji. Tibo i Tanja žive i rade na relaciji Beč - Slovenj Gradec. Cero je također u Sloveniji. Snježana je arhitektica u Londonu. Osim sa Snješkom, ni sa kim od njih nisam više u vezi. Od našeg studentskoga akustičarskog benda "Lucida Intervalla" (nastupi u KSET-u, Farmaciji, u Studentskom domu na Savi...) ostao je tek zapis na audiotraci.*

17. rujna 1991.

Jesam li potpuno svjesna svega što se u ovom kraju svijeta sada događa? Oko dva je poslijepodne. Ema spava i ne znam hoće li do kraja odspavati svoj poslijepodnevni san ili će ga prekinuti sirena za uzbunu i odlazak u podrum susjedne zgrade. Tamo smo noćas Ema i ja provele cijelu noć. Iako je službeno proglašen skloništem, spomenuti je podrum zgrade preko puta zapravo prostor neprimjeren sklanjanju: ispunjen je policama za registratore gornjokatskog ureda. Razmak je između polica tek tridesetak centimetara. Uklanjamo registratore, slažemo ih uza zid i, prekrivši daske dekama, spavamo između polica. Stiješnjeni kao - registratori. Je li to bilo jučer ili prekjučer? - da: u ponedjeljak - kako smo se S., Ema i ja zatekli, sasma slučajno, po prvi puta u skloništu, i to atomskom. Kad smo s Emom išli na pedijatrijski odjel bolnice radi Emina pregleda za upis u jaslice, oglasila se slabo čujna sirena pa smo zajedno s liječničkim osobljem i bolesnicima pohitali u sklonište. *U Zadru postoje tek dva ili najviše tri atomska skloništa! Tijekom rata ljudi su se spuštali u improvizirana skloništa (koja to nisu bila), drvarnice i podrume, u kojima su - događalo se - ginuli.*

Upravo čujem da je počeo napad na Biograd i da projektili padaju na samo središte mjesta. Misao o smrti stalno mi se vrzma po glavi. Molim anđele i svete da ne doživim Eminu nesreću, da ne budem očevicem nečega što ne mogu pojmiti.

18. rujna 1991.

Moji su sinoć boravili u našem stanu koji je navodno sigurniji od njihova, smještena na sedmom katu jugoistočne strane obližnjega nebodera. Proteklu ću večer zacijelo doživotno pamtiti. Proveli smo je u podstanarski skromno namještenoj kuhinji, u potpunom mraku. Jedino što je bilo živo u tom tmurnom i jezivom ambijentu bila je Ema (koja je navršila 19 mjeseci) i baterijski radio-kazetofon na koji smo pokušali snimiti par njezinih rečenica.

Ne znam kako je došlo do toga, ali u jednom sam trenu izustila da želim s Emom napustiti Zadar, možda čak i Hrvatsku. Tata je na te riječi skočio i stao vikati na mene prijeteći da će me se odreći budem li samo pomišljala na odlazak. Na njegovu viku ja sam reagirala još burnije. Vrisnula sam da želim zaštititi svoje dijete, da je tako malom djetetu nemoguće živjeti u ovim uvjetima: bez struje, vode, lijekova... Otrčala sam prestravljena u kupaonicu, a tata me je bijesan slijedio vičući za mnom da sam izdajica, izdajica svoje obitelji i svoje zemlje...

20. rujna 1991.

Krenule smo autobusom u Ljubljanu. Naš autobus bio je jedan od četiri ili pet koji su se istodobno uputili u Sloveniju. U našem autobusu, tik pored Eme i mene, sjedila je mlada žena s djevojčicom starom osam dana, u kutiji za novorođenčad. S djevojčicom kojoj nisu stigli nadjenuti ime.

Bila sam među prvima koji su ušli u naš autobus tako da sam mogla proučavati izraze lica ljudi koji su ulazili u vozilo. U mojoj je blizini pokušavala uz pomoć prijateljice sjesti jedna starica. Kako je to njoj išlo prilično sporo, neka žena pedesetih godina, koja je netom stajala iza starice, počela ju je gurati i vrištati. Među svim tim izgubljenim i suznim pogledima kojih vlasnici više nisu mogli ni na što reagirati nego se tek otisnuti na put (bez povratka?) - morala sam se pobuniti i doviknuti bezobzirnoj, podivljaloj ženi: "Zašto požurujete tu staricu? Zar zaista svi moramo biti ludi?"

Ema, moja Ema, sjedila je uz prozor i pozdravljala nonu i dida koji su stajali uz autobus. Još nije ni govorila. No, mnogo je toga razumjela. Znala se sa svojih šest zubića predivno smijati. Pitala sam se čuva li govor za neka bolja, mirnija vremena. Nona i dide smiješili su se kroza suze. Ili plakali kroz osmijeh. Bog zna hoću li vas ponovno vidjeti?, pitala sam se.

Cestom prema Pagu razmišljala sam o makiji pored puta i pitala se ne skriva li se možda u njoj kakav srpski ratnik. Približili smo se Paškom mostu. Na kamenjaru, pod suncem, u betonskoj baraci - stajali su gardisti. Prišli su autobusu radi kontrole. Pokazala sam Emi kako će prstićima načiniti slovo "V" za "victory". Naravno, ona je taj churchillovski pozdrav izvela loše i nespretno. Gardist je ipak razumio i nasmiješio se. Zatim mu je Ema poslala rukom "leteći" poljubac. Pomislih: malo radosti za tog bezimenog vojnika neizvjesne budućnosti.

Negdje pred Crikvenicom naš je autobus stao. Nešto je puklo u motoru. Čekajući drugi autobus, čuli smo s radija da su Zadar opkolili tenkovi, pa sam zaključila da je, uz već postojeću pomorsku blokadu, grad u klopci. Prisjećala sam se tate koji je moju odluku da odem nekamo s Emom dočekao veoma ružnim i pogrdnim riječima o mom kukavičluku, o strahu za sebe a ne za Emu... Taj prizor i moju histeričnu uvrijeđenost vjerojatno nikada neću izbiti iz glave.

Drugi je autobus stigao nakon sat i pol. Za to vrijeme razgovarali smo s radnicima na benzinskoj stanici. Strahuju da vojni brodovi pred Rijekom ne počnu gađati grad. Emi se na riječkom autobusnom kolodvoru smiješila ona mlada žena s bezimenom djevojčicom u kutiji. *Kasnije doznah da su djevojčici nadjenuli ime - Ema.* Na slovenskoj granici zaustavlja nas njihova policija i pita imaju li svi putnici osiguran smještaj u Ljubljani. Kažu: Ljubljana je prenapučena i ne može primiti više izbjeglica. Nude da ostanemo u Ilirskoj Bistrici. Dobit ćemo smještaj i hranu. Poniženost i bijeda... Svi putnici ipak nastavljaju prema Ljubljani. Tamo su prijatelji i privremeni dom u kojem ne vlada panika i gdje se ne čuje zavijanje sirena za uzbunu.

26. rujna 1991.

Nakon nekoliko dana provedenih u Ljubljani, kod prijatelja, Ema i ja avionom smo preko Klagenfurta otputovale u London.

1. listopada 1991.

U središnjem dijelu Westminsterske opatije, na najsvetijem mjestu u crkvi, u kapeli Edvarda Ispovjednik (Edward the Confessor) - utemeljitelja opatije, metar nasuprot drvenog krunidbenog stolca iz 1301. godine stoji natpis:

„Please pray: for all places affected by war and violence, especially Yugoslavia, and for those who work to make and maintain peace.“[1]

2. listopada 1991.
Rat, rat je tamo, u Hrvatskoj. Od jutra do kasno u noć sjedimo u Silvaninom stanu pred teletekstom iščitavajući najnovije vijesti iz domovine. Apsurdno je biti ovdje...

12. listopada 1991.
- Težak je put do demokracije - reče mi nepoznata, pretjerano našminkana postarija gospođa sjedeći meni nasuprot u vlaku londonske podzemne željeznice.
- Čuvajte se, *dear*. Željela bih ponovno u Dubrovnik...

29. listopada 1991.
Draga Snježana!
Već bi bilo krajnje vrijeme da ti se javim s nekoliko riječi. Ema i ja smo, kao što smo planirale, preko Ljubljane doputovale u Zagreb gdje boravimo više od tjedan dana. U Hrvatskoj je, kao što vjerojatno i sama znaš, stanje još uvijek konfuzno i sumnjam da će takvo uskoro prestati biti. Borbe ne jenjavaju a trenutno je i oko Zadra i Šibenika situacija prilično zategnuta i prijeti novim sukobima.
U Zagrebu boravimo u stanu koji je hladan, a kako smo sa sobom ponijeli samo najnužnije - živimo kao prave izbjeglice. Ničega od one udobnosti u Londonu ovdje nema. Srećom, imamo prijatelje, pa se snalazimo. Rekli su mi da će predavanja na zadarskom Filozofskom fakultetu početi vjerojatno 4. studenog pa se psihički pripremam za povratak u Zadar. Bilo bi mi zaista jako drago da se javiš. Veliki pozdrav.

H.

2. studenog 1991.
Taj mahniti zvuk sirene!
Sjećam se da nas je u noći kad se pretpostavljalo da će biti proglašena opća opasnost Pavuša nazvao i upozorio da je na radiju najavljena moguća uzbuna. *Ono što su Pavuša i njegov Zavod za zaštitu spomenika kulture radili tijekom rata, "krpajući" zgrade dan nakon što su granatirane - junački je podvig, koji se prebrzo zaboravlja !* Moji su te noći spavali u našem stanu. Ja sam nazvala neke ljude prenoseći im tu vijest. Nitko od

[1] "Molimo molite: za sva mjesta pogodena ratom i nasiljem, posebno za Jugoslaviju, i za one koji rade na stvaranju i uspostavi mira." (prev. s engl.)

nas nije znao kako će to izgledati, hoće li nas uistinu napasti, hoće li biti ruševina, poginulih... Strepili smo pred upoznavanjem toga čudovišta koje nam je zakucalo na vrata.

3. studenog 1991.

Nekoliko dana zaokupljaju me stihovi iz "Dulce et Decorum Est..." kojima Wilfred Owen sarkastično aludira na latinsku misao o slatkoj i časnoj smrti za domovinu. Strahote Prvoga svjetskog rata, koje opisuju engleski pjesnici njegova naraštaja, čine mi se dječjom igrom naspram onoga što se danas zbiva u Hrvatskoj.

Ovih dana palile su se svijeće na prozorima u Zagrebu. Preporučili su ostati kod kuće jer su groblja mete bombardiranja i mjesta na kojima bi općenito moglo doći do pucnjave. Ipak, za Svisvete i Dan mrtvih mnogi su ovdje išli na groblje. Bila je veća hrabrost učiniti to u Slavoniji, Dalmaciji...

Ema i dalje kašlje, nos joj stalno curi, nikako da joj prođe ova prehlada. Tako je hladno u Zagrebu! Budimo se kasno, poslije devet, kako bismo što dulje izbjegli hladnoću; pa ipak je i u taj sat - kako čujemo na vijestima s radija - temperatura na nuli. Jučer je u Zagrebu bila uzbuna oko 4 a danas oko 3 popodne. U oba slučaja na S.-nu sugestiju (ili naredbu?) nismo se sklanjali nigdje; ostajali bismo tu u stanu koji je na najvišem katu, pod pločom, bez krova.

Javnost je zaokupljena uglavnom onim što se događa u Dubrovniku, tako da je prekjučerašnji napad na Zadar na TV-vijestima jedva spomenut. Svaki puta, dok traje zvuk sirene za uzbunu, pred očima mi spontano prelete slike djece minom rastrganih tijela, djece u bolnicama, djece s velikim, preplašenim očima koje ne razumiju ništa, čak ne mogu u svojoj nemoći pitati: zašto? Vidim novorođenčad rođenu u podrumima bolnica, pored odraslih bolesnika, bolesnika s psihijatrije, traumatologije... Nekidan je u skloništu vukovarske bolnice (ili onoga što je od nje ostalo) rođena djevojčica Neža. *Djevojčica se rodila!* Je li taj prvi krik djetetov, krik novoga života, mogao obradovati Nežinu majku? Kako je to stvoriti život koji u plaču kriči udahnjujući ustajali podrumski zrak, kriči stravu i poniženje sićušna čovjeka koji je tu samo zato da bi se njegova pločica učvrstila u mozaik makropolitičkih i ideoloških previranja i interesa? Kakvi su to mehanizmi, strojevi za mljevenje mesa koji žrtvuju ama baš sve? Čak i život pred životom.

Novinarka iz Vukovara upozorava da su taj grad hrvatska javnost i hrvatska politika zaboravile. (Zar nije tako i sa Zadrom?) Dok se drugdje (bezuspješno) pregovara, u Vukovaru se gine.

Često mi na um pada Snježanin brat koji je sam odabrao vrijeme i način kako će okončati svoj život. Pitam se je li on predvidio sve ono što će se u nas dogoditi, sve ono što će se dogoditi u Zadru. Mora da sam Snježani još više otežala stvar svojim dolaskom i turobnim pričama o odlascima u sklonište. Primijetila sam da poprima osobine prave Engleskinje: odmjerenost i distanciranost. Vjerojatno je svjesna nužnosti da bude takvom, boreći se za posao i opstanak u prilikama sadašnje recesivne i inflacijske Britanije s gotovo tri milijuna nezaposlenih.

4. studenog 1991.

Albert Primorac... Na radiju obavijest i molba da se djevojka Alberta Primorca, koji je ranjen na Baniji, javi njegovoj majci. Albert Primorac... Koliko je takvih Alberta već ranjeno ili poginulo? Kolikim će Albertima biti upaljena svijeća ovih dana i svakog sljedećeg Dana mrtvih?

5. studenog 1991.

Ema i ja doputovale iz Zagreba u Zadar. Sutra počinje nastava na fakultetu. Uvedena radna obveza. Pitam se kako će godinu i po dana staro dijete u ovim uvjetima?

7. studenog 1991.

Danas je mamina i tatina godišnjica braka: trideset druga po redu. Zaslužili su mnogo vedriju obljetnicu.

(Mjesečnicu nisam dobila već dva mjeseca. A trudna mogu biti samo po Duhu svetom. Očito je došlo do strašne pomutnje u mom metabolizmu. Je li riječ o poremećaju prouzročenom stresom?)

19 . studenog 1991.

Opet je počelo. Opet su počeli...

Od jučer u 9.30 ujutro traje zračna i tzv. opća opasnost u Zadru. Ljudi bi trebali biti u skloništu. Počeli su s napadom na Nadin i Škabrnju a onda nastavili s artiljerijskim i zračnim napadom na Zadar. Jučer su iz Škabrnje odveli osamdesetak žena, djece i staraca u Benkovac, troje su na mjestu ubili. *Na sukošanskom groblju: šest grobova, jedan do drugoga, u crnom mramoru; grobovi mladića zaklanih u Škabrnji, s kojima je nekoć moj brat igrao košarku...* Jutros smo doznali da je u Zadru poginulo i ranjeno nekoliko ljudi a pogođena je i Sv. Stošija, Sv. Krševan, i brojne druge crkve i zgrade u Zadru. Što nas još čeka - Bog zna. *Sukošanska košarkaška ekipa danas loše stoji: nema naraštaja između kadeta i seniora.*

21. studenog 1991.
Četvrta obljetnica (propalog) braka.

24. studenog 1991.
U petak ujutro doputovali smo pod uzbunom u Šibenik. Čitavim putem bilo me je strah da nas ne pogodi granata ili ne zaustavi kakav srpski vojnik. Između Biograda i Pakoštana iznenada je iznad nas proletio jedan užareni projektil; sijevnuo je i šištao poput padajuće zvijezde. "Zaželi nešto!" - "Da ne poginemo."

U Šibeniku je relativno mirno. Borbe se odvijaju iznad Skradina pa uzbune obično oglašuju u sjeverozapadnim prigradskim naseljima. Boravimo kod S.-ih roditelja na drugom katu, pod krovom bez "ploče", ali u slučaju uzbune možemo ići dolje u garažu koja je ukopana u zemlju. Sutra bih trebala otići u Zadar, zbog posla. Ema će vjerojatno ostati tu. Mislim da je u Zadru trenutno mirno i da nije proglašena uzbuna. Međutim, tamo još uvijek nema struje i vode. Trebali bismo Emu sutra cijepiti ovdje, jer to zbog nedostatka struje ne možemo obaviti u Zadru.

Ja i ti u dva
grada-pobjednika
pobijeđeni pobjednici[2]

25. studenog 1991.
Postovani profesore Vidan![3]
U petak ujutro, pod uzbunom, odvezla sam se s obitelji u Šibenik kod suprugovih roditelja. I kad bih htjela ne bih Vam mogla pisati o tome kako je bilo u Zadru prethodnih dana. Dovoljno je reći da su, na putu prema Šibeniku, negdje kod Biograda, iznad nas letjeli projektili.

U subotu, u telefonskom razgovoru sa svojima doznala sam da je stiglo Vaše pismo s fotokopijom separata s beogradskog skupa. Ja sam objavljivanje tih naših referata već bila davno "otpisala", a eto - ipak smo i to dočekali i dobili, *via* Sarajevo. Otac mi je telefonski pročitao dio Vašeg popratnog pisma koje me je istodobno i ganulo i razveselilo. Hvala Vam na njemu. Što se tiče početka nastave na našem fakultetu, on je "do daljnjega" odgođen.

Ja međutim nisam cijelo početno zadarsko ratno razdoblje provela u tom gradu. Istoga dana, neposredno uoči blokade Zadra otputovala sam s malom Emom u Ljubljanu. Potom sam otputovala u London k svojoj sestrični. Provele smo Ema i ja tamo tri i pol tjedna. Znam, moj se

---

[2] Iz moga lirskog zapisa *Priča o dva grada*.
[3] Profesor Ivo Vidan bio je ugledan anglist koji je preminuo 2003. godine.

odlazak u Englesku u vrijeme kada po mom gradu padaju granate, pogibaju ljudi, a djeca poput moga stanuju u skloništu - može činiti izdajničkim činom. No, ja sam povrh svega htjela Emu zaštititi od nasilja, od njegovih slika i zvukova. (Ema običava svaku detonaciju popratiti upiranjem prstića u smjeru izvora zvuka detonacije i svojom dirljivom onomatopejom "dum-dum".)

Ne znam sjećate li se da sam Vam proljetos u svom pismu navela kako se nasilje odvija petnaestak kilometara od Zadra. Sada je ta udaljenost jednostavno poništena. ONI su došli do ruba grada, "tuku" nas danju, noću; počinju iznenada, ukidaju dovod struje i vode, ubacuju u lokalne radio-valove radio Beograd i Knin, ruše - kako oni kažu - "kamenje" naših crkava, romaničkih rozeta, renesansnih palača, baroknih koncertnih dvorana... *U lipnju 1999. konačno počela obnova posljednjega nesaniranog spomenika kulture u našem gradu - Kneževe palače...*; naše vinograde i maslinike pretvaraju u minska polja, a našim se mostovima igraju igre "Sad me vidiš - sad me ne vidiš"... Kolju, vješaju, od djece prave tjelesne i psihičke bogalje. Koliko traumatiziranih naraštaja? Koliko smrti, profesore? Koliko izgubljenih ljubavi, izgubljene nježnosti, roditeljske brige, koliko očajnih dječjih pogleda, i konačno: koliko poticaja za sućut od koje - kako piše Najveći u *Learu* - "možeš svisnuti"?

Srdačno Vas pozdravljam.

Vaša negdanja studentica,

Helena Peričić

27. studenog 1991.

Draga Jasenka,

nisam sigurna hoću li ti poslati ovo pismo. Čini mi se da sam ga u mislima napisala već stotine puta, a sada ne znam kako da sve to ispišem na papir.

Ovo što se događa nije dovoljno nazvati užasom (ili je riječ "užas" s vremenom izgubila na težini?). U Šibeniku je trenutno mir, ali i sama si iskusila kako se taj mir u hipu lako pretvara u pakao i razaranje. No, u svakom slučaju, stanje je takvo da se u njemu ne da ništa pametnoga raditi, stvoriti, ali se dade razmišljati i polako ludjeti. Pored moga je uzglavlja radio-budilica. Radio šuti a na satu su umjesto digitalnih brojki tek drečave, fluorescentno-crvene crtice i treptava točkica. Vrijeme je stalo. Ema pokraj mene spava. Na ormariću stoje izrezani novinski članci o razaranju Zadra, među njima i Pavušin iz *Dalmacije* od prošlog četvrtka. Šibenika mi je već pomalo dosta. Tu ništa ne radim jer nisam uspjela sa sobom ponijeti knjige. Nanovo sam pročitala *Leara.* Kriškovićem (moja potencijalna tema za disertaciju) apsurdno mi je baviti se ovih dana. Sve je apsurdno...

S.-u je rat pretvorio u mumiju koja od jutra do sutra čita novine: *Dalmacija - Nedjeljna i Slobodna, Danas, Newsweek*, gluparije, idiotarije (plagiram Aralicu)...

Čeznem za nježnošću, pažnjom. Ne dobivam ni zagrljaj, a kamoli poljubac. A kamoli još nešto "žešće". Sinoć sam nakon mjesec dana S.-i predložila seks. Nije čak ni digao pogled s novina. Gotovo je s odvratnošću promrmljao: "Hm?"

Voli te

Helena

28. studenog 1991.

Bila sam ljuta na S.-u kad je odbio da ga poljubim u kuhinji, nakon ručka. U prostoriji je osim nas bila samo njegova baka, no ona je u tom trenu prala suđe i bila nama okrenuta leđima. Naglo sam izašla iz kuhinje i ljutito zalupila vratima. Mislim da on ništa od toga ne razumije. Upravo sam mu to i rekla: "Mislim da ja čak tebe i razumijem, dok ti mene niti ne pokušavaš razumjeti."

Znam da je rat, da se umire, da masakriraju čak i djecu. Znam da je S. užasnut mogućnošću novačenja. Ali: zar moram baš svakoga časa na to misliti? Zar nemam prava, kao i bilo tko drugi, sebi dopustiti da barem na časak zaboravim svu stravu i da se barem privremeno, trenutno, prividno isključim iz svega toga? Uostalom, treba mi nešto što će mi uliti barem malo snage za sve ono što predstoji?

Da bi donekle ublažio svu napetost među nama, S. me je predvečer odvukao u kupaonicu gdje smo pružili sebi stanovit luksuz ljubljenja u trajanju od dvije minute.

25. prosinca 1991.

Ja sam s Emom na nekoliko dana došla k bratu u Split. Noćas su mama i tata sa susjedima jeli bakalar pod svijećom, u hodniku ispred lifta (to je, recimo, "najsigurniji" prostor na sedmom katu njihove zgrade). Granate su pogodile veliki broj stambenih zgrada na Voštarnici.

30. prosinca 1991.

--- u porušenoj dvorani
među relikvijama blještavila i baršuna
crni klavir
po kojem smo nekad
dječjim prstima

prosipali (neshvaćeno) Chopinovo domoljublje
hrvatske poloneze sviraju negdje drugdje---

25. veljače 1992.
S. otišao na brod. Ostavio nam je društvo granata.

19. svibnja 1992.
Upravo je otkucalo osam navečer na susjedinom satu. Po tko zna koji put palim svijeću. Maločas sam po tko zna koji put nazvala Jasenku. Dosađujem joj telefonom. Noćas je bilo gadno u Zadru. Poginulo je šestoro ljudi, među njima i jedna djevojčica. U ulici M. Oreškovića. To mi je kazala profesorica Brozović. Po tko zna koji put Ema i ja otpjevale smo „Moja domovina". I pitam se: koliko još puta? Koliko još besmislenih puta?

26. svibnja 1992.
Sumrak. Beethoven iz stana u zgradi preko puta. Tajnoviti zvuk klavira isprepliće se s detonacijama iz Dračevca. Ili možda Bibinja. *I danas se sjećam mušmule pod gazdaričinim balkonom i one zvjezdane večeri. Osjećam miris lišća i plodova. Doista. Koliko sam u međuvremenu, od upravo te večeri, osjetila, osjećala? Koliko se u međuvremenu od mene očekivalo ljubavi i mržnje?*

Vijesti iz Sarajeva. Arkan umro. Zar? Atentat na Šešelja. Neuspio. Gađaju sarajevsko rodilište u podrumu kojega je uz majke smješteno 170 djece. Pitam se: gdje je granica ljudske bestijalnosti? Koje su još metode ubijanja i mrcvarenja neotkrivene? Koja je količina mržnje potrebna da se zakolje žena s djetetom u utrobi?

29. svibnja 1992.
Večeras sjedim sama za stolom, uz lumin i petrolejku. I buljim u Snježanino londonsko, mirisno pismo. Ruke su mi ljepljive i htjela bih snom ukloniti taj neugodan osjećaj. Ali san neće na oči.

Cigareta? Ne: zlo mi je od nje. Glazba na radiju - loša. Pričekat ću "Kroniku dana". Petrolejka šišti. Sjene slika na zidovima siluete su mojih starih (prežaljenih?) ljubavi. Gospode, htjela bih živjeti drukčije! Pokušavam napraviti svijeću od ostataka starih. Idiotski posao. Vlažna, predkišna večer. Rojevi muha u kuhinji. Prisjećam se onih isto tako vlažnih, sivkastih prijepodneva u Londonu, kada nebo visi nad gradom a iz jeftinih talijanskih i indijskih dućana kuljaju mirisi čajeva i začina...

30. svibnja 1992.

RIĐAN I TRI IVANA
(tri priče o nasilju)

Jahač na riđanu, s mačem u ruci, jaše u punom galopu.

Radio: *svjedoci - žrtve - izvršiteji.*. Pitam se postoji li mjerilo mržnje, sustavnost nasilja, protuteža zlu. Čak je i onaj vlastelin iz Jasne Poljane, koji je pokušao dokučiti zakonitosti rata i mira, davno zapisao kako bi želio živjeti a *ne stražariti* nad vlastitim životom.

Grančica mirte u jednostavnoj staklenoj vazi zaprepašćuje me svojom ravnodušnošću.

* * *

I. priča

Svibanj 1967.
Zadar, Park Vladimira Nazora

Tukli su ga. Dvojica. Toga se dobro sjećam. Jedan ga je, doduše, samo pridržavao ispod pazuha kako bi ga onaj drugi mogao bez pogreške udarati u lice i trbuh. Šakama. Nisu se čuli glasovi. Tek tupi udarci i stenjanje.

Naša je "teta" naglo prestala razgovarati s voditeljicom druge grupe i, okrenuvši se prema nama, žurno rekla:

"Pogledajte, djeco, ono stablo s blijedožutim cvjetićima. To je mirta. Mirta prekrasno miriše."

Ne znam jesu li drugi pogledali mirtu. Sumnjam. Ja zasigurno nisam. No, ona mi se zato uspjela nametnuti svojim teškim, preteškim mirisom. Tamno zelenilo i svježina parka u čas su prestali izgledati pitomo i zaštitnički. Sada je to bilo mračno i zagušljivo mjesto s kojega je trebalo što prije uteći.

Hodali smo dvoje po dvoje u povorci. Nijemo. Većina pognute glave. Primijetih da su ona dvojica napadača iznenada nestala ostavljajući na zemlji pretučenog. Kada smo mu se primakli on je već pokušavao ustati. Posrtao je i teturao. Konačno se naslonio na stablo i, pritiščući rukom trbuh, počeo povraćati. Iz ustiju mu je curilo nešto što me je tada, viseći onako do zemlje, podsjetilo na duge tamnocrvene najlonske niti kakve je ujak koristio za udice.

Ivan je hodao sa mnom u paru. Držali smo se za ruke kao što to za šetnje čine djeca u vrtiću. Primijetio je da netremice promatram pognutog mladića pa mi je prijekorno stisnuo ruku.

"Glupa si!", rekao je Ivan i prstom pokazao tetu.

Miris mirte postupno se u meni preslikavao kao neumoljivo nadolaženje plime gnušanja i mučnine.

Pomislih u jednom trenu kako Ivan ništa ne zna.

On zaista NIŠTA NIJE ZNAO.

II. priča

Studeni 1991.
Selo nedaleko Zadra

Tata je upao u kuću. Rekao je mami da uzme Katu. Čuli su se pucnji i zvuk motora. Bio je to kamion. Znam sigurno. Katarina je počela plakati. Ona je još mala. Ja sam veliki.

Tata je iz najviše ladice u ormariću za cipele izvadio neku kuvertu. I nož. Uzeo je crnu plastičnu kesu za smeće i u nju utrpao odjeću. Nije mu smetalo što ga promatram. Kada se žuri tata ne voli da mu se motam oko nogu. Tako on kaže.

Onda me ščepao za ruku. Svi smo istrčali na dvorište. Odatle smo čuli strinu Rosu kako viče: "Ljudi! Ljudi!" Onda su se čuli krici. Pa stenjanje. Tata i mama s Katom u naručju potrčali su prema polju. Ja sam gledao kako nestaju. Onda se tata osvrnuo i kriknuo:

"Ivane, sine, jesi li lud? Zašto ne trčiš?"

"Ne mogu, tata", rekao sam. "Ne mogu se maknuti."

Tata me zagrlio. Imao je velike oči. Onda me uzeo u naručje i pojurio za mamom i Katom. Nosio je mene i plastičnu crnu vreću; kuverta i nož bili su mu u džepu. Tata je gubio dah i šaptao:

"NIŠTA TI NE ZNAŠ, moj Ivane. I bolje da ne znaš..."

III. priča

Svibanj 1992.
Zadar, naselje Voštarnica

"Udri ga, Majo, udri! Jebeš mu mater. Kako ti ne znaš! Eh... Prema njemu ne treba imati milosti."

Mlatili su ga plastičnom cijevi iz koje je tekla voda, vukli su ga, rastezali mu udove, prskali mu vodom oči, gurali glavu u vrećice sa smećem, da bi konačno krenuli k otvorenim vratima drvarnice i, stavivši mu glavu između vratiju i dovratka, pokušavali je prikliještiti, smoždíti.

On je zavijao, cvilio. Raskrečenih nogu stajao je pred vodom preplavljenim dvorištem. Kao Mojsije pred Crvenim morem. Čekajući čudo izbavljenja.

Djevojčica je vrištala u transu rituala mučenja. Kao kakva voodoo svećenica. Ivan ju je poticao i korio što je odviše milosrdna. On je bio glavni u dvorištu. Možda i u kvartu. Imao je psa i znao je kako s njim. On je sve znao.

Ovaj je Ivan ZNAO SVE.

* * *

Perpetuum mobile (ne)spoznavanja zla. Oko deset uvečer. Pod svijećom. Eksplozije u daljini. Pod krovovima. Pod očnim kapcima. U mozgu.

Zadnje vijesti: *svjedoci - žrtve - izvršitelji...*

Jahač na riđanu jaše u punom galopu.

Grančica mirte i dalje je sablažnjivo ravnodušna.

22. srpnja 1992.

Predala zahtjev za rastavu braka. *Moja Ema oca nije vidjela godinama. Ne znam što se to ljudima događa. Ne znam što se meni dogodilo.*

5. rujna 1992.

- O čemu se radi, gospodaru?

- I z m e đ u koga?

Sjećam se da je moja baka Marija, rođena u Mravincima ponad Splita, potkraj svoga života, zatečena i prestravljena zlom koje je sve više uzimalo maha, da je ta moja baka Mravinka, koja nije mogla izreći riječ "jogurt" već ju je izgovarala kao "jorgut" - da je govorila kako se bliži - USU SVITA.

I ta moja baka Mravinka, koja je cijeli svoj život provela glave pokrivene rupcem - a u starosti joj je crni rubac prekrivao kosu bjelju od snijega - ta moja baka govorila je da se bliži - USU SVITA. Ta moja baka, koja je svoje posljednje godine provela na omrznutom sedmom katu nekakve betonske grdosije - jer na selu više nije bilo nikoga tko bi je mogao paziti (ili ona njega), ta moja baka govorila je kako se bliži - USU SVITA.

Ta moja baka, koja mi je kao djevojčici plela pletenice natapajući ih pljuvačkom (jer je ona to sebi radila kao mlada djevojka u vrijeme Prvoga svjetskog rata) - a čega sam se ja onda pomalo gnušala, ta moja baka, pametnija od Salamuna, govorila je da se bliži - USU SVITA.

Bog je dao (rekla bi ona) i moja najdraža Mravinka nije dočekala da vidi ni djelić onoga što je onako razočarana nagoviještala.

* * *

Tjelesno, površinsko, krvavo nasilje koje ljudski um, koliko god bio staložen, ne može pojmiti i upiti a da ne poluči gnušanje i zgražanje kao jedinu moguću obranu (kako ne bi šenuo i potpuno onemoćao) - to nasilje nije jedino koje nas u ovim vremenima dočekuje raširenih ruku. Nasilje se možda skriva i u mnogo manje vidljivim pojedinostima: u porama i česticama ljudskoga življenja, koje nisu tako očite i opipljive.

Jer, valja se sjetiti i svih naših mizernih bogatstava koje smo nosili u torbicama ili plastičnim vrećicama u drvarnice, podrume i skloništa, ili smo ih - ostajući u vrijeme oglašene uzbune u stanu - držali uza se kao nešto što nam treba uvijek biti pri ruci jer je to esencija našega života ili nas samih? Svi ti dokumenti s potpisima i pečatima, nešto zlatnine i par pisama, fotografije sa zajedničkog izleta, sve naše tektonske a prividnim ravnodušjem zakrabuljene strasti i čežnje za životom... No, je li nas rat naučio da taj isti život cijenimo više no što smo ga cijenili ranije? Oni zagrljaji koje smo po završetku uzbune jedni drugima srdačno i gotovo ludi od sreće darivali izlaskom na svjetlo, na sunce, na svakodnevnicu - postupno su se pretvorili u svoje mefistovsko naličje: neimaština, zavist, ogorčenje, cinizam, osvetoljublje, vlastohleplje... Skrivajući pred sobom vlastite pogreške i grijehe postajemo "kršćani" koji se živo križaju i prečesto prizivaju Njegovo ime noseći u sebi tek jednu vjeru: kako je Bog sebi prvom bradu stvorio. Prisjećam se osmrtnica čija ganutljivost traje koliko i novine - tek jedan dan; prisjećam se studentica u crnini - koje tuguju za kolegama-studentima; djece koju (usprkos svemu!) valja ponovno učiti dječjim igrama... No, to kotrljajuće zrnje *naše* svakodnevnice udarit će o zid onih idiotskih živciranja proizišlih iz bog-zna-čega; one blaziranosti spram tuđega jada pretvorena u nepažljivo odslušan trač; onog bagateliziranja nesreće za jednu etiketu više prosrpstva, prokomunizma, projugoslavenstva, prohomoseksualizma, promiskuiteta, prostitucije... A sve to konačno će natkriliti snažno, nepokolebljivo i nadasve nadmoćno seciranje, mrcvarenje, optuživanje i osuđivanje u (pre)dugim novinskim napisima. Nevidljivi, papirnati a tako "smjeli" suparnici umjesto kamena bacit će jedan drugom u lice rukavicu izazova (igrajući se uljudnosti na razini verbalnih svinjarija!) da bi prave žrtve po završetku toga dvoboja bili zapravo oni koji će te njihove novinske stupce čitati - sekundanti *passa tempa* (tobože) povrijeđene taštine, sekundanti intimnog, istinskog USU SVITA.

- *Mislim, o čemu se radi u knjizi koju čitate, moj kneže?*
- *Same k l e v e t e, gospodine...*[4]

13. rujna 1992.
Prisjećam se Budimpešte.
Prisjećam se svjetla koje se prosipalo po ogromnim mostovima nad Dunavom. Ispijala sam bijelu kavu u maloj restauraciji uza široku ulicu u središtu grada. Činilo mi se da njihovi restorani nisu onako konfekcijski i luksuzno uređeni kao što je to slučaj s većinom restorana u Zagrebu i malih kavana u primorju. Budimpešta! Ležala je pred nama kao kakva polugola Toulouse-Lautrecova plesačica. (Nije li "plesačica" secesionistički, nepotrebni eufemizam za "bludnica"?) Ipak, bila je zanosna ta Budimpešta, s natrpanim izlozima - ušnim resicama nemilosrdno opterećenim teškim jeftinim naušnicama; sa zastorima na prozorima - zgužvanom čipkom na nabreklim dojkama; s fluorescentnim plakatima kojima se blijedo oponašalo blagostanje zapadne Europe a stizalo tek do predgrađa s luna-parkom ograđenim šarenim žaruljama. Eh, Budimpešta! Pokraj nas mirisali su svježi kolači (kakvi se spravljaju samo u tom gradu: s orasima, marmeladom od borovnica ili prelivenim lavom od čokolade...) Htio je da mi tamo bude dobro. Trudio se: bio je mladi ljubavnik koji strahuje kako će svakog trena u nečem pogriješiti. Bio je zbunjen i smeten, rijetko što bi uspio izvesti kako je namjeravao. Ali baš zato bio je drag i, gotovo do suza, ganutljiv.
Plašila me vlastita razmaženost i hirovitost, moć da zatražim što hoću, nadmoć koja pred djevojkom može prijateljski prekriti činjenicu da ta ista djevojka počinje zalaziti u ono što nazivaju - opasnim godinama.

3. listopada 1992.
Rastava braka.

1. studenog 1992.
Noćas je Zadar napustio jedan od najperspektivnijih zadarskih glumaca -lutkara - Srećko Šestan. Ne znajući kamo bi s njom, svoju je staru "ponicu" ostavio meni. On svojim odlaskom a ja prihvaćanjem darovanog

---

[4] Citati su, dakako, preuzeti iz *Hamleta*.

bicikla - nehotice smo sami sebe uvrstili u, tih mjeseci već oformljenu, gardu ratnih profitera.

13. studenog 1992.

Mrlja

Na bijelom stolnjaku mrlja od vina.
Ja kažem crvenog, ti tvrdiš crnog.
Ti tvrdiš crno, ja kažem crveno.
Crno kao: "nebulozno", "nisam znao", "tenzija"...
Crveno kao: "trebam te", "patim", "priležnica", ...

Crno i crveno stopljeno u mrlju.
Ti tvrdiš crno, ja kažem crveno.
Crveno i crno razliveno po horizontali dušja i ravnodušja.
Crno kao:"javit ću se", "imam posla", "pretjeruješ"...
Crveno kao: "javi se", "obožavam te", "u vražju mater"...

25. studenog 1992.

CARPE DIEM
(priča o njemu i njoj)[5]

Želi mu reći sve. Nema vremena. Odlazi. On. *U ponoć.*

- Ja...

On joj poklopi dlanom usta. Vidjela mu je donje zube. Bili su požutjeli od nikotina. Bili su to najljepši zubi koje je vidjela. Ona pomisli da šizi.

On joj začepi usta poljupcem.

D. H. Lawrence. Grozničavost. *Carpe diem.* Uhvati dan. *Ne: uhvati sekundu. Djelić sekunde!*

- Ljutiš se na mene?, upita ga Ona dok mu je pomagala nositi putnu torbu. U pet do dvanaest. Kamen je na Kalelargi bio sklizak. Pet do dvanaest.

- Ne, rekao je. *Ili možda samo odmahnuo glavom.* Ona se više ne sjeća.

U stvari, bila je sretna. Fraza? *Ne. Možda kao nikad dosad. Nikad* ***dotad.*** *Bože, ta to je već ... Past tense. Kao nikad. Barem ne u posljednjih*

---

[5] U ovoj priči kurziv je sastavni dio diskursa.

trideset godina. On joj ne vjeruje. Kako da joj vjeruje? A mogla je. A dogodilo se. Usudila se. Zaiskrilo nešto.

- Javit ću ti se.
- Nadam se.
- Eh, kad ti kažem...

Galantni muškarci. Kurtoazija. Ljubaznost. Povlađivanje. Nije valjda.

- Ali, pisati mi možeš...

Što? Sentimentalna pisma, patetične bljuvotine. Diletantsku literaturu. Tatjana piše Onjeginu. A zna se kako je to završilo. Dobila ona nogu. Spasiba. Djevuška. Djevojčura. Bez ponosa, dostojanstva. Tako nekonvencionalno. Glavom u zid. Besramno.

- Ne boj se. Dolazit ću.
- Ne bojim se, samo proživljavam ovo što mi se dogodilo. Što NAM se dogodilo.

On je poljubi.

- Ti si tako divno sentimentalna, reče On i okrene leđa.

Što misliš tko si!, htjede kriknuti Mefistofeles**,** *Počela sam obožavati, ogoljena do srži, a ti si to obožavanje frcnuo kao mrvicu sa stola...Take it or leave it.*

- Zašto si pobjegla? Čekaj!

On iskapi neko crveno piće. Stao je pričati o sebi, o ljudima oko sebe... Vrijeđalo ju je što ga vrijeđaju. Čula je svaku petu riječ. Razumjela svaku desetu.

Bila je pijana. Od njega. Od sreće. *Ah, trivijalnost. O terminu: trivijalna literatura - P. Pavličić ili M. Solar? Bog zna. Sreća je trivijalna stvar.* Govorila je gluposti. Bila sentimentalna. Ruke su drhtale.

Teško je disala, bez riječi, **nesposobna** da izusti riječi. Napokon reče:

- Zašto ti to meni pričaš? Čemu opravdanja. Pa ja ti se divim!

On je pogleda u oči. Ona pomisli da tone. *Precioza.*

- Daj mi ruku, reče Ona.

Ruka zagrlila ruku. Prsti se isprepleli.

Njezina se ruka polako oslobodi zagrljaja. On joj micanje ruke poprati pogledom.

Našla GA je. On putuje za jedan sat. Možda nešto više. *Ah: više. Pa to je cijelo bogatstvo. Taj jedan sat. Ali to nije važno. To što putuje.*

Pogleda ga. Dodirne mu prstima obraz. On joj uzme tu ruku i pritisne je na svoja usta.

Teško je disala.

- Bojim se da će ovo ujutro izgledati tek kao san, reče mu Ona.
- Ta ovo i jest san, reče joj On.

Samo san.

U egipatskoj grobnici pronašli gusjenicu. Izišavši na zrak nakon tisuća godina životinja se pretvori u leptira. Ogromnog, šarenog, sedefasto-ljubičasto-tirkiznog. Oživje leptir. Živje sat. Možda nešto više. Ta to je čitavo bogatstvo. Onda ugine. Spržen. U hipu.

Što misliš tko si!, htjede kriknuti Mefistofeles, *Počela sam obožavati, ogoljena do srži, a ti si to obožavanje frcnuo kao mrvicu sa stola... Take it or leave it.*

- Imam puno posla, doprlo je iz slušalice.
- Čuješ li ti mene?, upita On nakon kratke stanke.
- Da, tu sam.

O njemu ništa nije znala. *Obožavam ga.*

Teško je disala.

- Ne, ne mogu ti reći. To je delikatna stvar. Nemoj se ljutiti. Reći ću ti to u četiri oka. Kad dođem...

Galebovi su udarali krilima o prozor sobe na zadnjem katu. *Lude.*

Kompjutor je zujao. Svjetla na otocima zatreperila.

Danas kao da je netko sunce prekrio crnom krpom. Iznenada. Iz inata. Dišpet. Kada ćemo se konačno ponašati kao Dalmatinci?

Ogolila se do srži. On joj ne vjeruje. Njoj. Toj ženi. *Frustriranoj. Sumnjivoj.* A njezini interesi? *Interesi!? Bože blagi.*

Dodatak nakon završene predstave? Gluma, pomisli Ona i stisne zube.

Ali ja nisam čovjek od teatra, za Brechtovu teoriju ne dajem ni pišljiva tri groša, ja se ne mogu distancirati, ja ovo DOŽIVLJAVAM, ovoga časa, do dna, ja, ja, ja, ovo sam ja, čovječeee! Opsjednuta sobom. Opsjednuta tobom. Ovo mi se ne događa svakih petnaest dana. Ili mjesec. Kao menstruacija. Kao neki psihosomatski poremećaj.

- Treperim. Ah, trebam te. (*Tako banalno, tako istinito.*)

- Daj mi volje, snage, to je jedino što tražim, reče Ona. Želiš osvojiti svijet? O.K. Pomoći ću ti da ga osvojiš. Daj mi snage i ja ću osvojiti svoj. Ovaj mali. Kakav-takav. Ali moj. Daj mi snage i dat ću ti je. Čuješ li. ČUJEŠ LIIIII? Dakako, misliš da je ovo ludost.

Folie.

- Imam posla, doprlo je iz slušalice, Pa ne mogu se ponašati kao pijani...

Bez završetka rečenice. *Ti telefoni...*

Nemoj da izustim ono što mi se otima iz grudiju. Hoće kriknuti u noć. Da udari krilima o prozorsko staklo na najvišem katu. Kao galeb. Da se rasprši među treperavim svjetlima na otocima.

Kao san.

Kalvarija. Nada. Restaurant "Roko". I njegova braća. Strast. Snaga. Seks. SEXplicite. Ševa. Ooo-da ševi. *P. B. Shelley.*

Bože blagi. Umirem.

- Ti si tako divno sentimentalna, reče On i okrene leđa.

Kao san.

ZAISKRILO NEŠTO. Leptir. Sedefasto-ljubičasto-tirkizni. Spržen. U hipu.

Carpe diem.

28. studenog 1992.

(na sastanku mog Odsjeka na Filozofskom fakultetu)[6]

Ja: Htjela sam se nadovezati na prof. D-a. Riječ je o "korektnim međuljudskim odnosima". Molim dakle određene osobe koje su mi uskraćivale pravo na knjige iz knjižnice Zavoda i pri tom kazale da ih idem tražiti na drugom mjestu, "s obzirom na moje ponašanje", da to više ne čine.

Lady Macbeth: Kolegice Petričić...

Ja: Peričić, gospođo, Peričić... Isprva sam htjela da mi to netko objasni, no ubrzo sam zaključila da je razlog u glasovanju. Ne samo da sam bila

[6] I dan danas prilike na lokaciji opisanoj iz davne 1992. nisu se mnogo promijenile. Ljudi na akademskim pozicijama imaju, čini se, odviše slobodnoga, intelektualnog vremena i nekonstruktivne energije tako da se oni vrlo često troše na konstrukcije, spletkarenje i podmetanja. "Hrvatski jal" začet je, vjerujem čvrsto, u akademskim gnijezdima. Unatoč njihovoj takozvanoj humanističkoj profiliranosti.

uvrijeđena, nego upravo šokirana. A sve to samo zbog suzdržanog glasa u raspravi o postupku kolegica koje su uočile neke nepravilnosti na ispitima; samo zato što sam se s njima solidarizirala i suzdržala se od glasovanja...

Pesak (tobože iznenađeno): Pa Vi se, kolegice, imate pravo suzdržati...

Ja: Kolega Pesak, ponavljam - zbog suzdržanog glasa...

Lady Macbeth (za sebe): Vi mislite da ste najgenijalnija osoba na Odsjeku... (Kolegici iz Makedonije rekla je da se ponaša "balkanski", da se vrati u Makedoniju, i da bi trebala naučiti kako se u Zadru valja ponašati /??!!/. Ja sam prošla bog-bogova: "sofisticirano"!)

Lady Macbeth: Ali ja sam rekla...

Ja (povišena glasa, pred eksploziju): Molim Vas, gospođo knjižničarko...

Lady Macbeth: Ja sam odobrenje za Vaše zaposlenje tipkala...

Ja: Ja to poštujem i na tome Vam zahvaljujem...

Columbo: ... A ja sam ocijenio i potpisao...

Ja: Pa valjda ste, profesore, za to imali nekakva razloga!!!

Nakon "fešte", u hodniku, dr. Fox mi namigne, a Smišna-kovrčava pošalje mi rukom kroz zrak poljubac.

(Dr. Fox: Od one pobune 1992. ništa se na Odsjeku ne da popraviti.)

4. prosinca 1992.

Bog.[7]

Postajem egocentrik. Po svemu sudeći, to sam oduvijek i bila. (Za poslove kojima se ti i ja bavimo vjerojatno je nužna prilična količina samoljublja.) U ovom gradu čovjek živi kao nekakav primitivni organizam, koji samoga sebe ždere. Hrani se vlastitim staničjem, vlastitim tkivom. Dok se ne potroši. Od prvoga trena nudim ti svoje povjerenje, makar znam da tvoje još nisam uspjela (hoću li ikad?) dobiti. Sva ta podozrivost koja je bliska ženama (ali i muškarcima) što u ovim stvarima taktiziraju i kalkuliraju doživljavajući zavođenje (hoćeš-nećeš: to je to!) kao neku diplomatsku misiju - meni ide na jetra. Mislim da je to tek blesavo prenemaganje. Ja se tako ne znam ponašati. Nisu me dovoljno "dobro" odgojili. Ti mi ovo možeš vjerovati, ali i ne moraš. Sve što sam ti dosad o sebi rekla - istina je. *Možda upravo oni koji ne posjeduju neophodne (ili suvišne?) mehanizme distanciranja izazivaju sumnju. Ima uostalom ljudi koji misle da je Medeja bila tek nastrana, histerična baba, a Ema Bovary jeftina kurva, zar ne? Ne znam razumiješ li me, ali se nadam - ako utvrdim da sve ovo prezireš - kako mi se neće dogoditi da mi, kao u onoj priči, doviknu: "Car je gol!"*

---

[7] Pismo koje nikad nisam poslala.

Doznah da si na putu. Oprosti, povremeno mi je potrebno čuti te. Bilo mi je to jako važno upravo ovoga tjedna.

Pokušavam raditi što više mogu. U posljednje vrijeme tako bih rado radila nešto "svoje", ali ne smijem. Moram raditi ono što moram. To mi oduzima silnu energiju. To se (svjesna sam toga), odražava i na moj odnos prema Emi i prema drugima. Jednostavno, ovo mi je obveza, Sizifov kamen, a i tema disertacije nevjerojatno je zahtjevna. Na faksu sam ponekad i do šest navečer. Ranije sam posuđivala fakultetski kompjutor odnoseći ga vikendom kući, ali sada dolazim subotom na faks. Voljela bih tu ostajati i noću (moram se zaokupiti nečim!), ali ne smijem zanemariti Emu.

Ona je božanstvena. Kad to kažem razmišljam o njoj kao o djetetu uopće, a ne samo ***svom*** *djetetu. Navečer, kad usne, promatram je, onako mirnu, sklopljenih očiju i pravilna disanja, i onda sa strahopoštovanjem pomislim kako je u šutnji i snu tih krhkih, dječjih tijela - neizmjerno dostojanstvo i nadmoć. (Kao u sfinge koja čuva rješenje neke fatalne zagonetke.)*

Laka noć ti. Lijepo sanjaj. Čuvaj se.

(Ja nisam čovjek kakvim si me sebi predočila – rekao je...)

28. prosinca 1992.

Osjećam se
kao da mi je netko izvrnuo dušu
poput džepova kaputa,
pa ih sada siječe škarama
kako u njih više ništa ne bi stalo.
Happy New Year!

29. prosinca 1992.

Što misliš, što bih sve dala da se ponovi onaj tvoj pogled koji se dogodio jedne večeri u predvorju kazališta i trajao možda čitavih šest-sedam sekundi? *Pogledi... Jorgovanić...*[8] Da barem ovo nije samo dio igre pravila koje ja uopće ne znam!

30. prosinca 1992.

Postala sam nepoćudna osoba. Možda bi me se morao kloniti. I nemoj onako "često" nazivati telefonom: to bi te moglo *skupo* stajati.

Možda čak i žeton tjedno. Pet impulsa.

U arteriji.

---

[8] Rikard Jorgovanić, hrvatski književnik (1853.-1880.)

31. prosinca 1992.

U nedjelju navečer pokušala sam se opiti. (A inače ne pijem.) No, to mi je samo djelomično uspjelo. Bio je to prvi pokušaj u životu. Vrbnička Žlahtina... U "Basketu"... Poprimam postupno kavanske manire zadarskih intelektualaca...

Bog zna što će za par mjeseci od mene biti. Možda bi bolje bilo da me prije toga pregazi auto.

20. veljače 1993.

Osamdeseti rođendan maestra naše književnosti, prvoga živućeg hrvatskog pera - Ranka Marinkovića: „Rat. Rat je nešto mnogo strašnije nego svi njegovi simboli..."

15. ožujka 1993.

Dobila pismo iz Vatikana od Monsignora C. Sepea, u ime Ivana Pavla II., kao odgovor na moj apel upućen Papi, za zaštitu Hrvatske. *Znate li koliko se ljudi od spomenutog datuma do danas okoristilo svojim "domoljubljem". Neki od njih ulaze danas među "200 bogatih hrvatskih obitelji", zar ne?*

18. ožujka 1993. (Radio-emisija *Usprkos*)

NAJAVA: Dva su tjedna od posljednjeg *Usprkosa* iza nas. Bilo je bure, južine, a ponekad bi okrenulo i na "Orkan". No, tim vremenskim i inim nepogodama usprkos, mi smo vam pripremili novu emisiju...

- Borise (*Boris je i danas jedan od najduhovitijih a zasigurno najugodniji glas zadarskog etera.*), znaš li koja je razlika između Lesi i Dalmatinca?

- Nemam pojma. Koja?

- Lesi se vraća kući, a Dalmatinac nikada.

25. ožujka 1993.

Dragi Pavle[9],

da ti pravo kažem: ne znam odakle da počnem. Kako vidiš, pišem ti na kompjutoru. Svom, čovječe, vlastitom. *Macintosh Classic*. Koji traje dok ima struje u Zadru. A nje više nema nego ima.

Nadam se da se ti dobro oporavljaš. Bila sam na promociji tvoje knjige. Pretpostavljam da su ti Edi i Šenol već podnijeli "izvješće".

Dopusti nešto o mojoj malenkosti: meni se u posljednjih pola godine mnogo toga (a možda i malo toga) dogodilo. Početkom listopada uspjela

---

[9] Pismo je pisano Pavlu koji je tih dana kao invalid Domovinskog rata boravio na liječenju u SAD.

sam se razvesti. O tome ne bih nadugo jer je to činjenica za koju smo on i ja podjednako krivi. Jednostavno, ja sam povukla prvi potez jer više onako nisam mogla nastaviti. Sada sam sama. To mi u ovim ratnim danima prilično teško pada jer poželim da mi barem netko stavi ruku na rame i kaže: Bit će sve O.K. (Pa makar me taj i zavitlavao.) A ni glumiti vedrinu (čitaj: majmuna!) pred Emom, dok trideset metara od nas padaju granate, nije baš jednostavno.

U posljednje vrijeme pokušavam u ovom gradu nešto napraviti. Počela sam na radiju Donat FM uređivati i voditi jednu emisiju pod naslovom *Usprkos* (kultura, književnost, studentski život - dakle sve ono čega u Zadru - nema). **Usprkos** svemu. Gotovo sve priloge pišem sama. Vidiš, mogao bi mi ti napisati koji prilog i poslati. Stvarno, javi se. Piši o čemu god hoćeš. A dok budeš pisao misli na to da ću tvoj tekst čitati oko deset navečer, sjedeći leđima okrenuta pola metra udaljenom (otvorenom) prozoru, koji je jedino što me dijeli od sjeveroistoka. A ti znaš što k nama iz toga smjera dolazi. Vampiri se bude upravo oko deset navečer.

Drugo, pokušavam pokrenuti među kolegama (a i studentima) jedan književni časopis. Sve je to u povojima (danas se kaže:"pampersicama"!) i možda bi bilo bolje o tome ne pričati. Znaš i sam kako u Zadru završavaju sve inicijative: zatiru ih u korjenu. Oni koji bi mogli nešto poduzeti, nastave sjediti u naslonjačima i govoriti kako bi - "nešto trebalo učiniti". U sukobima između Grada i Županije - ne zna se čiji je ovo grad.

Uporno nastojim nešto učiniti od svog života (koji je u posljednje vrijeme poprilično jadan). Mislim da ću - ako mi se u dogledno vrijeme nešto poticajno ne dogodi - otići k vragu. Krahirati ću, časna riječ. U svakom pogledu. Ovaj grad *kills me*, čovječe. U protekla dva dana za petoro sam ljudi čula da odlaze iz Zadra. Neki od njih u Novi Zeland. A takve me vijesti "podižu", mo' š mislit'? Polako se davim u ovoj močvari priglupog entuzijazma.

Sjećam se vremena kad smo pisali za *Fokus*. Gdje je onaj zanos, čovječe?

Iščitavam ovo pismo i divim se sama sebi kako mogu nekoga ubijati u pojam svojim pisanijama. (I to nekoga tko je preletio "baru" da bi se liječio u Americi.) A što ćeš? To ti je tako kod nas. Iz perspektive nekog drugog grada (ili kontinenta) stvari u Zadru izgledaju sasma drukčije. Mi smo Zadrani za sve ostale luđaci. A to možda i nije daleko od istine. Tko je ovdje još normalan?

Slušaj, javi se. Bilo bi mi drago. I svakako napiši nešto za *Usprkos*. Nemam pojma što je s Irenom. *Stvarno, što je s Irenom?* Ja ti se inače nikome izvan Zadra ne javljam. Jednostavno, ne znam što bih tim ljudima rekla.

Čuvaj se. Znaš što bi kazala moja stara: Pamet u glavu, Pavle! I oporavi se. Par prstiju više ili manje na ruci, kao da je to bitno. Uostalom, prsti i ne služe ničemu osim da ti kroz njih procuri ovo malo sreće.

Bog.

31. ožujka 1993.

U Jelsi na Hvaru preminula dr. Marija Brida, sveučilišni profesor u mirovini, hrvatski filozof i humanist. Veći dio svoga radnog vijeka provela je na Filozofskom fakultetu u Zadru. *Tek nakon dugo, predugo vremena na zadarskom je fakultetu konačno upriličena komemoracija. Jesu li posrijedi bili ideološki razlozi? Ili možda svjetonazorski?*

("Ja imam svjetonazor a ideologiju mijenjam svake tri godine, što je normalno. Prema tome, ja nisam ništa kriv : kriva je moja ideologija!"- tako ljudi danas razmišljaju.)

Uskrs 1993. (Radio-emisija *Usprkos*)

UVODNO SLOVO:

... Ovo što ste upravo čuli pjesmu „Jeruzalemski dijalog“ Miroslava Krleže. Riječ *Uskrs* nije teško izvesti iz riječi *Usprkos*. Sretan vam i miran bio ovaj dan i ostatak blagdana.

Ovo je dakle ekskluzivno, prigodno izdanje *Usprkosa*. Ako kojim slučajem, usprkos "bogatom" kulturnom životu u Zadru, slušate ovu emisiju, s vama će biti dugokosa, šarmantna ton-majstorica Sandra, jedan od najljepših glasova u Zadru a i šire - Gordana-Goga zvana *Georgia on my mind*, i opaki materijalist (koji ovo sve radi za silnu lovu, čitaj: zabadava!), vještica i urednica emisije - Helena. Ako vam se, dakle, sviđa takvo društvo, ostanite s nama sljedećih sat ili nešto duže.

Inače, vi nemate pojma koliko mi vas volimo. Upravo vas - koji čak i Uskrs provodite u ovom gradu u kojem se ne živi nimalo udobno; vas - koji čučite u svojim sobama pokraj radija, i ne gledate čak ni televiziju, nego štrebate za sljedeći ispit i grickate uskrsnu pogaču. Volimo **vas** koji ste ostali na Uskrs tu, u ovom gradu, u koji struja ne stiže, ali stižu informacije da će ona poskupiti šezdeset posto.

Ali, i u svom tom zlu ima nečeg dobra. Sjetite se samo koliko ste novih ljudi upoznali u ove dvije godine otkako ste prisiljeni čekati u redu za vodu i crni kruh, ili dok u podrumu (ako uopće idete tamo!) dodajete slane štapiće, igrate briškulu ili prepričavate novi nastavak *Svete Barbare*. (Jeste li zamijetili: scenografija američkih TV-sapunica uključuje izrazito kvalitetna, masivna vrata?)

No, kao što ovaj veliki dan treba čestitati vama - slušateljima, tako čestitke treba uputiti i ovom našem gradu koji je, kao i njegovi stanovnici, kroz mnogo toga prošao i prolazi. Treba i njemu zaželjeti da se njegovo vlastito uskrsnuće što prije dogodi.

A mi sada, za Uskrs, poslušajmo Mahaliju i pjesmu "Happy Day" koju smo i u prošloj emisiji dok su na grad padale granate - slušali. Slušali granatama usprkos. Jer zapravo: nijedan *Usprkos*, Uskrs i nijedan "Happy Day" nije suvišan.

19. travnja 1993. (Radio-emisija *Usprkos*)

NAJAVA:

Dobra vam i ova večer u emisiji *Usprkos*. Nismo se čuli od Uskrsa pa vam imamo večeras reći dosta toga. Nadam se da ćete i večeras biti s našom šarmantnom ton-majstoricom Sandrom (*Babac*), s Antom (*Tomićem*) i urednicom emisije Helenom. Ako kojim slučajem tijekom emisije začujete neke čudne zvukove koji dolaze odnekud s neba, iz sjeveroistoka, ne dajte se zbuniti: to su samo provokacije. (Za vašu utjehu, mene od sjeveroistoka dijeli samo prozor, i to otvoren.) Prostor od Zadra do Šibenika tek je neurotično područje koje se dade provocirati.

Uostalom, da nije riječ o provokacijama tim bi se zvukovima pozabavili Zagreb i međunarodna zajednica. A oni su, razumnjivo, pametniji od nas: znaju ljudi što rade. I stoga: ne dajte se provocirati. Jer, ovo je emisija *USPRKOS*.

UVODNI KOMENTAR: Od Uskrsa do danas mogli smo nazočiti raznim kulturnim zbivanjima u Zadru. Tri književne večeri održane od 14. do 16. travnja u Hrvatskoj kazališnoj kući, predavanje prof. Ive Banca, premijera kazališne predstave "Sveti Roko na brdu", nova predstava zadarskoga Kazališta lutaka na Marulovim danima... Pa „tko reče da ovoga grada nesta?", zapitao se jednom pjesnik. O svim spomenutim zbivanjima bit će govora u emisiji.

A sada par riječi o nečemu što se ovih dana *nije* događalo u Zadru.

Naime, u utorak 20. travnja započeo je nakon prilično velikih porođajnih muka u Hvaru a onda se nastavio u Dubrovniku, 59. međunarodni kongres PEN-a. Kongresu (jer, prema riječima predsjednika PEN-a Gyrgyja Konrada: to je ipak kongres) nazočilo je oko 400 članova iz tridesetak zemalja. Mnogi PEN-centri nisu poslali svoje predstavnike. Tako je zbog pomanjkanja kvoruma kongresu oduzet radni karakter i na njemu se nisu mogle donositi revolucije... pardon - rezolucije. Mnogi "daklem" nisu došli. Tako nije došao ni ruski penovac, pisac i veeeliki humanist Limonov. A da je on stigao možda bi mu se pridružili također pisci i veeeliki humanisti Vuk Drašković i Dobrica Ćosić. Jer pisci su humanisti i savjest svijeta. A hvala nebesima što u ovom slučaju ne moramo imati na savjesti ovakvu *savest*. Neka se takvom *savešću* diči netko drugi.

Gospoda književnici doputovali su udobnim brodom iz Venecije na Hvar, a u srijedu su udobno doputovali u Dubrovnik, i nakon udobnog i razdraganog druženja i svađanja na kopnu i moru, oni su se udobno vratili domu svome. Kao da Fritz Beer nije upozorio da je "intelektualno udobna egzistencija neizbježna smrtna postelja idejama".

Podsjetimo da je prije točno šezdeset godina na kongresu PEN-a u Dubrovniku, dakle 1933., u vrijeme buđenja nacizma, sudjelovao poznati britanski pisac i socijalni prorok - Herbert George Wells. Iste je godine Wells postao predsjednikom svjetskoga PEN-a naslijedivši preminuloga Johna Galsworthyja. Upravo je Wells bio čovjek koji je u članku "Mogućnosti propasti civilizacije" još 1909. predvidio opći tijek događaja u slijedećih 30 godina. On je glavne uzroke propadanja svijeta vidio u pretjeranom naoružanju i financijskoj nesigurnosti, a jednom je rekao da je "Moderno (je) ratovanje ludost a ne razuman poslovni pothvat". Bio je to također čovjek koji je svojim književnim djelima anticipirao znanstvenu fantastiku suvremenog tipa. Tako jedan njegov roman toga žanra nosi naslov "Rat svjetova". A u smislu dolarskog utržka važno je taj roman spomenuti kao predložak za poznati film "Rat zvijezda". Da se kojim slučajem mister Wells digne iz groba mogao bi vidjeti da ni *science-fiction* nije ono što je nekad bio, da je znanstvenu fantastiku njegove vrste prekrila prašina, i da se u ovom kraju svijeta događaju toliko fanstastični ratovi svjetova koje ni on u svojoj mašti nije mogao zamisliti.

Mi gospodi PEN-ovcima želimo ugodan povratak kući. Ratu svjetova usprkos.

ODJAVA: I tako, došli smo do kraja i ove emisije *Usprkos*. Studenti koji se ovdje povremeno javljaju svojim prilozima produžili su, čini se, svoje uskrsne blagdane. Znam, ovdje postaje prilično **neudobno** živjeti. Ali mi smo tu upravo usprkos. Možda će do sljedeće emisije biti bolje. Mislim, manje neudobno.

Moram prije kraja emisije zahvaliti Sandri i Anti što su me podnosili. Pozdravlja vas urednica i voditeljica emisije s uobičajenim pozdravom: Makar se radilo o zvijezdama od projektila - ne idite maleni ispod zvijezda!

Po broju listova koji su izlazili u raznim hrvatskim mjestima do 1920., grad Zadar odmah je iza Zagreba. Samo na hrvatskom jeziku bilo je do te godine 82 lista, a izlazilo je još listova na talijanskom jeziku i nešto na njemačkom i latinskom. Za nepunih 150 godina, tj. za 147 godina, uključivši i vrijeme između dvaju ratova, u Zadru je izlazilo ili još izlazi

112 listova na hrvatskom jeziku. To je značajan broj, koji bi bio daleko veći da poslije Rappalskog ugovora dvadeset i jednu godinu nije bilo onemogućeno da u Zadru izlazi i jedan hrvatski list.

7. svibnja 1993.
Fascinira me misao/činjenica kako je potrebno boraviti tek dvije stotine kilometara sjeverozapadno ili zapadno odavde da bi se živjelo drukčije. Da se ne mora udisati zrak binarnosti: ima te ili te nema. Kako je moguće da samo zemljopis određuje elementarnu egzistenciju?

8. svibnja 1993.
Sinoć je u Zadru održana premijera predstave Mirka Bogovića pod naslovom *Stjepan, posljednji kralj bosanski* u izvedbi ansambla Kazališta lutaka u Zadru. Tomislav Durbešić, redatelj, u prigodnoj riječi uz predstavu napisao je: "Ne kažem da je ova tragedija Bogovićeva ni dobra ni loša, ali ima jednu neprocjenjivu vrijednost: ona je na tragu, u ono doba, mukotrpnog traženja izraza, na mladom hrvatskom jeziku, svih tajnovitosti i jezika i ljudskog bića". Redatelj je također našao prednosti ovoga Bogovićeva teksta u analogiji zbivanja u Bosni sredinom 15. stoljeća i zbivanja sadašnjih. Stoga, valja čestitati našem malom ali svjetskom Kazalištu lutaka na predstavi tijekom koje smo držali palčeve jer smo strepili da je ne poremeti ili prekine zvuk kakve granate. Ova predstava zasigurno će s vremenom postati sve dorađenija i bolja. *Predstava je u doživjela samo dvije izvedbe jer su tijekom jednog skorašnjeg granatiranja iz spremišta, stražnjeg dijela Sv. Dominika, ukradeni svi skupocjeni kostimi i maske.* Zasada pak možemo reći da su zadarsko Kazalište lutaka, Durbešić i Mihatov osvarili ako ne objektivno veliku predstavu a ono ipak značajnu predstavu vrijednost koje se ne može mjeriti tek teatarskim aršinom.

9. lipnja 1993.
"U našoj zadarskoj svakodnevnici, koja uglavnom traje do dva popodne, u kojoj su mnoge bitnosti izgubile na težini, u kojoj čak i smrt - koliko god bila ili baš zato što jest česta - postaje tek suhoparna konstatacija, mi ćemo večeras slušati upravo o onim pojedinostima, onim značenjima pohranjenim u gotovo već zaboravljenim česticama življenja, u treperavim svijećama (čovjekovim) koje u okruženju blještave i bučne pirotehnike začudo još uvijek gore i ne dadu se utrnuti. I zato, dok u ovom našem vremenu i prostoru, pojedinac postaje tek povijesnim obrascem, svojom predvidljivošću doveden do vulgarnosti klišeja, mi se susrećemo na večeri poezije..."

Dva sata nakon što izgovorih ove riječi na predstavljanju najnovije zbirke jednoga zadarskog pjesnika, sjedila sam u društvu s još desetak "ljubitelja poezije" na terasi Ribljega restorana u zadarskoj Foši. Noć je bila vedra, obasjana zvijezdama. Noć, činilo se, kao i mnoge druge u Zadru početkom ljeta. Čavrljanje i hihotanje vinom potaknutog društva iznenada je prekinulo šištanje nekih novih zvijezda koje su nas stale prelijetati i padati u more, tek stotinjak metara od nas. I kao da nas to nije neugodno iznenadilo, već smo taj ruski rulet doživjeli kao originalnu zabavu. Iz restorana sam telefonom nazvala svoje. Bili su silno uznemireni i tražili da se, ponajviše zbog Matovilke, koja je zbog potreba mojega profesionalno-stvaralačko-neplaćenog angažmana te večeri, morala noćiti kod mojih, na jugoistočnoj strani sedmoga kata "nebodera", jedne od granatama najizloženijih stambenih zgrada u Zadru - hitno vratim kući.

Ostala sam s društvom još neko vrijeme (prethodno umirivši svoje riječima kako se "ništa posebno loše neće dogoditi"). Vozeći se sama "peglicom" prema Voštarnici, nisam osjećala strah (iako su me granate imale "na tanjuru"): prisjećala sam se sličnih situacija kad bi tijekom predavanja oko podne "zvijezde" padale u more tik do fakultetske zgrade koja se nalazi na "najljepšoj rivi na svijetu", dok su mene i moje kolege na samom vrhu zgrade pomno slušali "najluđi studenti na svijetu". Boraveći kod mojih u takvim trenucima, obično u vrijeme ručka, začuvši detonacije Matovilka bi, u kuhinji okrenutoj "suncu i zvijezdama", hitro sišla sa stolice (na kojoj je prehodno sjedila "na petama"), i odlučno zgrabivši tanjur sa stola, odjurila onim svojim kratkim u široke hlače obučenim nožicama ka dnevnom boravku, tobože "najzaštićenijoj"[10] prostoriji u stanu, i - položivši tanjur na stolić - nastavila slasno jesti. Kao da se ništa dogodilo nije.

2. listopada 1993.

Slatka Irma (djevojčici iz Sarajeva)

- ... - reče Pas i ugasi olovnu cigaru na Irminim leđima.
- Ne pitaj me ništa, dijete - rekla joj mati čas ranije.

Pas ispuhne dim, a majku više nitko ništa nije pitao.

11. studenog 1993.

Bilo je oko deset navečer. Granate su šištajući prelijetale autobus, kao padajuće zvijezde.

- Zaželi nešto - šapnem sebi.

---

[10] Tijekom rata u Zadru pokazalo se da nijedna zgrada i nijedna prostorija nije zaštićena: ljudi su ginuli i u podrumima.

Nitko od mojih nije znao da sam na putu. Primicala sam se gradu koji je bio pod uzbunom. Samo da me nitko u autobusu ne prepozna, pomislih. Lažna ljubav i rat - plitka ali opipljiva metafora za Eros i Thanatos. Trebao mi je. Zagrljaj. Nakon nekoliko sati ležala sam mu okrenuta leđima. Osjećala sam se jakom, štoviše nadmoćnom. Dobila sam ono što sam htjela: privid topline i prisnosti. Bez poljubaca, naravno: jer su mi se gadili. Pri pomisli da se ujutro vraćam kući, *incognito*, osjećala sam olakšanje. Jer: vraćala sam se kući. U grad koji je bio - pod uzbunom.

28. studenog 1993.
Vjetar i posljednji Mohikanci (*Narodni list*)

Gospodin Daniel V. dobrohotno očekuje članak. Gospodin Daniel Day-Lewis glumi posljednjeg Mohikanca. No, krenimo redom.

Krenuli smo redom. Družba "Posebne vožnje" za "Dane Zadra" u Zagrebu u ponoć 26. na 27. studenog u autobus je primila nekoliko vojnika koji su se uputili prema Maslenici. Među njima bio je jedan 23-godiπnji dobrovoljac gusarskog izgleda, s rupcem na glavi, Spličanin. Nekad bih ga nazvala Mandrilom, ali sad neću. Pričao mi je o tome kako se, kad je doma u Splitu, sa ženom i djecom, želi što prije vratiti na teren. Dok se rat ne okonča ne želi raditi ništa drugo. Samo, napomenuo je, kad bi drugima bilo malo više stalo do onoga što radi on, πto rade svi njemu slični koji se noću uvlače u neprijateljska sela i ne znaju hoće li se vratiti. Nisam sigurna je li mi povjerovao kad sam mu rekla da cijenim to što čini. Namjerno ga nisam pitala za ime. Nisam htjela znati ime. Mogao se zvati Golijat, ili David, ili Roland - svejedno. Splićo je izišao iz autobusa. U noć. Bog zna..., pomislih ne želeći dovršiti misao.

* * *

Dakle, "Dani Zadra" u Matici iseljenika u Zagrebu. Ili putovanje blokiranom cestom do metropole. A čini se da je put do nje blokiraniji no što smo očekivali. Najprije smo nešto iza ponoći prelazeći - većina od nas po prvi put u životu - pontonski most gledali na videu u neobično dobro opremljenom autobusu dokumentarac o razaranju Zadra. Vozač autobusa kasnije je obrazložio: "Da se podsjetimo". Pitam se međutim, je li na završnoj večeri "Dana Zadra", kako je bilo najavljeno, film o ratnom Zadru doista prikazan. Pretpostavljam da tamošnje ljude nije potrebno podsjećati. U Karlobagu smo, čekajući deblokaciju ceste i blagoslov prometnika, dok se autobus nemilo njihao na ledu i vjetru, gledali igrani film pod naslovom *Vjetar*. Pretpostavljam, opet, da se podsjetimo...

* * *

Kažu da je završna večer predstavljanja estradno-pjesničkog staralaštva ratnog i nepokorenog Zadra - uspjela. Zadar je grad dostojanstvenih ljudi. Koji nikad neće priznati poraz.

U Zagrebu te dostojanstvene ljude dočekuju očima punim sažaljenja i, recimo, razumijevanja. Kao što se promatraju traumatizirana, napuštena, asocijalna djeca koja mogu prirediti nešto nepredvidivo, napraviti scenu. Takvu djecu konačno ne treba shvaćati ozbiljno. I svakako im se (djeci) mora oprostiti. Ne znam je li itko na "Danima Zadra" spomenuo podatak o sedam zadarskih samoubojstava u mjesec dana. Ako nije, pretpostavljam da razlog leži u opasnosti od poremećivanja estradno-poetskog koncepta predstavljanja grada koji ovih proteklih godina nije klonuo duhom.

Prisjećam se članka o posjetu Zagrebu, objavljenog prije dvije godine. Malo se toga promijenilo. Jedino, onda se pisalo o netom srušenom mostu, a sada valja pisati o pontoncu.

Zagreb je bio i ostao dalek. Put do njega i preko njega blokiran. Npr., nije jednostavno prijeći trg pokraj željezničkog kolodvora. Tamo se na očigled kralja Tomislava gradi višekatnica pod zemljom. Kamen po kamen. Kamen smutnje za potencijalne regionaliste, autonomaše, anticentraliste. Izazov prgavim, neposlušnim Dalmatincima koji poslušno ostaju u Dalmaciji. Ali, oni se ne daju isprovocirati podzemnim građevinskim čudom na čijem će vrhu umjesto krova biti zasađeno ukrasno bilje.

Na putu prema Zadru gledali smo nastavak filma o razaranju zadarskog kraja. Kasno poslijepodne na dionici Senj - Karlobag bilo je više no sumorno. Vrhovi brda uz cestu bili su zaklonjeni oblacima. Kao da dim cigareta kulja kroz prozore autobusa i obavija brda. U daljini se nazirao natpis s nazivom gostionice. Na ekranu tijela Škabrnjana prekrivena plastičnom crnom folijom.

"Ručak!" - veselo uzvikne Tome. Trgnem se. Trun u oko. "Ručak... ručak... ručak....!", odjekuje u glavi. Škabrnja. U blizini parkiranog autobusa šepavi pas. Dim cigareta i dalje obavija oblake. Budite milostivi, nemojte više ništa dodavati...

Nakon što je većina utažila glad, i žeđ, započela je na videu projekcija filma "Posljedni Mohikanac". Daniel Day-Lewis, Hamlet s predratnog Lovrijenca i sin Cecyla, engleskog autora prelijepih stihova o ratu (ako se o ratu uopće može pisati lijepo) - bio je Oko Sokolovo. Crnokosi, koštunjavi Mohikanac ili Hamlet odvratio je pogled od barba Ivanove kuće u Rovanjskoj, kuće kojoj su iskopali oči. Na mjestu negdanjih prozora sada su mračne duplje. Kad se barba Ivan, i Mate, i Ante budu vraćali u Rovanjsku i Novigrad, valjalo bi ići s njima. Vidati rane osakaćenim kućama. Vraćati im vid. Mislim da po krovovima kuća nećemo saditi ukrasno bilje.

Konačno, prelazimo pontonski most. Po drugi put u životu. Nije to doduše blještavi Golden Gate, ali je to naš, ratni, mračni i zamračeni most nade. Dok je put do Zagreba trajao petnaest sati, povratak je bio znatno kraći: tek 9 i pol sati. Naš će autobus biti jedini koji će te večeri stići iz metropole.

* * *

Gdin. Daniel V. dobio je članak. Gdin. Daniel Day-Lewis odglumio je posljednjeg Mohikanca. Autobus je vozio ususret svjetlima velegrada, istinske metropole na sjeveru Dalmacije.

Vraćali smo se. Mi - prgavi, gorki, dostojanstveni ljudi.

Posljednji Mohikanci.

JELE[11]

17. prosinca 1993.

S vremena na vrijeme bacim se leđima na (pre)veliki gazdaričin bračni krevet sa starim "šustama", i stanem u polumraku sobe zuriti u strop osvijetljen tek svijećom. Ema je u susjednoj, dnevnoj sobi, usred hrpe igračaka razbacanih po ostarjelom, olinjalom tepihu. Rat, samoća, hladnoća, dijete s upitnom budućnošću u susjednoj sobi... Grlo mi se steže.

Danas (vidiš: to je zanimljivo) kao da je gorčina negdje na pregibu jednjaka nalik onoj iz prošlih vremena. Od pustih mi se domoljubnih i inih licemjera želudac diže. Poželim zašutjeti a ne buncati koješta a sve kako bih vlastitu glavu održala iznad površine vode umišljajući da svo to krzmanje ima smisla...

Jebite se.

18. prosinca 1993.

Kula babilonska (*Narodni list*)

- Htio si, priznaj!
- Priznajem...
- Htio si učiniti nešto za ovaj Grad?
- Jesam...
- Htio si mrtve dići iz groba?
- Jesam...
- Htio si mi malo glumiti Krista, ha?

---

[11] Pseudonim kojim sam potpisivala kolumnu u *Narodnom listu*.

Entuzijast slegne ramenima:
- Jesam.
- E pa onda odglumi Krista do kraja!
Vrag ode tresnuvši za sobom vratima.
Entuzijast ostane sam. Kao i uvijek.

* * *

Bio jednom Grad. U njemu su živjeli Entuzijasti i oni koji to nisu. Entuzijasti odlučiše sagraditi kulu do neba. Zato su potražili pomoć Ne-Entuzijasta. Ali Entuzijasti i Ne-Entuzijasti govorili su različitim jezicima i nisu mogli razumjeti jedni druge. Jezik Entuzijasta bile su njihove ideje, jezik Ne-Entuzijasta bili su novac i moć. Entuzijasti su mislili da je u glavama Ne-entuzijasta želja za novim zamislima, a Ne-Entuzijasti - iako su se busali u prsa svojom odanošću novim idejama - bili su uvjereni da je u glavama Entuzijasta želja za novcem i moći. Jedni u druge projicirali su vlastite mehanizme razmišljanja. Postupno se napetost među njima povećavala. Javili su se i zavidnici i konkurenti - među Entuzijastima kao i među onima koji to nisu. Dobre nakane zatirane su u začetku. Uz to, prijateljstva su kopnila, neprijateljstva se nemilosrdno množila. Gradu je prijetila katastrofa. (A taj isti Grad tijekom stoljeća othrvao se i kugi i gladi i ratu.)

U Gradu je nastala galama: Entuzijasti su uzvikivali svoje ideje, Ne-Entuzijasti su upirali prstom u devizni tečaj i lupali šakom o stol. Konačno je zavladala panika, a Grad je, nakon više tisućljeća svojega postojanja, zbrisan s lica zemlje. Kula nikad nije sagrađena.

Grad se **nije** zvao Babilon.

* * *

- Htio si, priznaj!, drekne Vrag.
- Jesam... - reče Entuzijast.
- Vrag ti nije dao mira...

Entuzijast ustane i, tresnuvši za sobom vratima, izađe iz Grada.

JELE

23. prosinca 1993. (Božićni broj *Narodnog lista*)
Tako je - ako vam se čini

„Dobro jutro, dragi slušatelji. Ekipa naše radio-postaje želi vam sretan Božić i ujedno vas podsjeća da je u tijeku dvjestočetrdesetineki dan opće opasnosti..."

Ovu su rubriku urednici (bez mog znanja a kamoli dopuštenja) naslovili "Zrcalom zbilje". (Pirandello se vjerojatno okreće u grobu zbog ovog naslova.) Uz dužno poštovanje prema onom tko je odabrao naslov, priznajem da sam zatečena. Jer, zrcala ne volim, a što se tiče zbilje - nisam načistu s time što ona uistinu jest. No kako glede mimesisa nisu bili načistu ni mnogi mudraci, počam od Aristotela do Auerbacha (žive ostavljavljam na miru, jer o njima: samo dobro) - zaključujem da nisam pozvana da baš ja budem načistu. Pridržavam stoga autorsko pravo na svoju varijantu zbilje i njezina preslikavanja. Usput, upozoravam, ukoliko ste vi - koji niste načistu sa zbiljom - okruženi onima koji su uvjereni da znaju što je zbilja - to vam se lako može razbiti o glavu. Ali to je tema neke druge priče. Ili nekog drugog razbijanja glave.

Nedavno je jedan Zadranin, koji to više nije jer je prije stanovita vremena napustio Grad idući trbuhom za kruhom (ili kruhom za trbuhom), izjavio kako je "(...) gore gotovo isto kao u Zadru; jedina je razlika u tome što se tamo ne puca". Najprije sam pomislila da nisam dobro čula, ali ubrzo shvatih da sam - dobro čula. Čovjek je misao izrekao prilično ležerno, gotovo utješiteljski. Antologijska izjava bila je izrečena toliko uvjerljivo da automatski pomislih: "Istina je, čovjek je u pravu. Pa isto je, nema razlike." Ali se onda u glavi javi Post Scriptum koji je glasio: "Pogotovu nema razlike ako uzmeš u obzir da je čovjek - otišao iz Zadra." I tada sam ustanovila da je moja zbilja definitivno drukčija od zbilje dotičnoga gospodina.

Dovršavajući prethodnu rečenicu začujem kako nešto fijuće i udara. Ne u zaleđu, ne na periferiji, već tu. Možda baš u blizini onih ljuljački na igralištu u Jazinama; možda upravo uz kazališnu zgradu, u kojoj su se djeca jutros mogla igrati lego-kockama i pogledati božićnu predstavu. Tu negdje, sasvim blizu. Ovdje, u glavi, u prsima. A jedan mi je kolega jednom rekao kako s gledišta fizike stvari izgledaju vrlo jednostavno. Od trena kada začuješ zvuk ispaljenja računaš otprilike tri sekunde. Upravo toliko vremena imaš. Nije to ništa. Ne pogodi li te ona prva, mala je vjerojatnost, ako se u one tri sekunde negdje skloniš, da će te pogoditi druga. Stvar se dakle može do krajnje mjere pojednostavniti. Sve se dade racionalizirati. Onaj fijuk običan je zvuk mase i brzine. Nije to ništa. Tresak i prašina - prirodne su, fizičke posljedice udarca tj. snage. Ako se problem racionalizira, ostaje vam vrlo malo mentalne i emocionalne energije za strah, tjeskobu, za iščekivanje nakupljano tijekom posljednje tri godine, za bijes... A da o ljubavi i mržnji (ako ne-daj-bože nekoga mrzite) i ne govorimo. Tri godine rata zgusnu se u tri sekunde vaših izgleda za opstanak. Čista fizika. Nije to ništa.

* * *

Približava se Božić, dan opraštanja i blaženog darivanja ljubavi. Prisjećam se znančevih riječi: "Gore je isto..." Vrlo je jednostavna, kažu, ova naša zbilja. Fizikom objašnjiva. Ona ne luči zlobu i zavist, ne iziskuje sućut. Ali, u ovoj našoj zbilji žaruljice u izlogu svjetlucaju (dok ima struje) drukčijim sjajem negoli tamo gore - gdje je isto. Ovdje se klinci u Jazinama njišu drukčije negoli tamo - gdje je isto. Ovdje je zagrljaj djeteta i stisak ruke o Polnoćki drukčiji negoli tamo - gdje je isto. I stoga mislim da u onom znanstvenom obrazloženju nešto nedostaje: naša se sentimentalnost ipak ne da objasniti fizikalnim zakonima. Niti se fizikom može objasniti naš Božić.

Sretan vam *naš* Božić, dragi Zadrani.

Makar bio takav - kakvim vam se čini.

JELE

3. siječnja 1994.
Stigla je... (*Narodni list*)

Na početku ovoga članka kao i nove godine dužna sam čitateljima jednu ispriku u ime naših tiskara - sadašnjih, a pogotovu onih bivših - ispriku za sve one tiskarske greške koje su morali trpjeti u prethodnim napisima *Narodnoga lista*. Primjer takvog napisa bio je i božićni članak u ovoj rubrici. Zaista je zanimljivo kolika je moć tih tobože nevažnih "tipfelera": u trenu oni mogu izmijeniti autorov "lični opis", svjetonazor pa i nacionalnu pripadnost. A da i ne govorimo o grotesknim semantičko-sintaktičkim kombinacijama i aluzijama koje iz tih tiskarskih gremlina proizlaze. Uz ovu ispriku vezana je i novogodišnja želja upućena našim slovoslagarima da u ovoj i narednim godinama budu što bolji u svojemu poslu.

* * *

Stigla je, dakle. Deset godina nakon Orwellove 1984. stigla je Ona, tajanstvena, obasuta zvjezdanom neizvjesnošću, ganc-nova - 1994. godina. Svatko do nas kročio je u nju s najboljim željama za sebe i svoje bližnje, ostavljajući za sobom onu bolećivost neizbježne rekapitulacije koja nas obuzima tijekom božićnih i novogodišnjih blagdana, rekapitulacije svega što je u protekloj godini učinio - ili nije, postigao - ili nije.

* * *

A doček Nove godine započeo je za neke domjenkom *Narodnoga lista* u restoranu *Marina*. Neočekivani (pre)veliki broj uzvanika ulijevao je, iskreno rečeno, prije strah negoli strahopoštovanje. Bio je to osjećaj koji je moguće rezimirati u pitanju: tko će to sve platiti? Možda bi se upravo pisac ovih redaka mogao uvrstiti u prekobrojne jer je od domjenka ili, točnije, od uzvanika bezobrazno očekivao nešto drugo. Sama proslava, večera i program bili su u granicama korektnog jer, razumije se, ljudima je povremeno potrebna prigoda koja će ih razveseliti i barem nakratko potisnuti nelagodu uzrokovanu ratnim okružjem. Međutim, u odjelu za prekobrojne čula se i poneka biserna primjedba. Tako su oni koji su ili odveć navikli na luksuz vlastitoga doma ili im pak taj luksuz toliko nedostaje primijetili kako ne mogu piti vino koje se ne toči iz boce od sedam deci. Onima koji su po hrvatskim hotelima smješteni ne kao gosti već kao beskućnici vjerojatno bi te ili novogodišnje večeri pasalo i vino iz jednolitarske boce. I tako, večer u znaku najstarijeg tjednika na Balkanu nije mogla proći i bez lucidnih balkanskih primjedbi. Ali, možda to valja shvatiti tek kao "tipfelere" te večeri. A te se večeri razgovaralo i o ljudima - doduše više o ženama nego o muškarcima - pa se moglo zaključiti kako je čovjeku dovoljno par dana bez granata da počne više ili manje uvjerljivo pripovijedati o onima koje površno ili uopće ne poznaje. Pričalo se i o poslu, pače su se i nadobudno dijelile posjetnice. A sve to uz poneki vic, pa i pokoju psovku... Tako je te večeri bilo je očito da su se muškarci, u svojoj namješteno ležernoj ulozi poslovnih ljudi, trudili biti muškarci, a žene su, u uobičajenoj ulozi statista, nastojale biti žene. Preveliki broj uzvanika a opet, čini se, premalo i muškaraca i žena.

I tako je i ove godine stigla godina od koje se očekuje da bude Nova.

JELE

23. siječnja 1994.

"Pobjeda" braće Lumiere (*Narodni list*)

Pri pomisli na kino "Pobjeda" nikad mi, iskreno rečeno, nije bilo jasno o kakvoj se tu pobjedi radi.

U subotu sam otišla u kino. Po prvi puta nakon rata otišla sam u zadarsko kino, jedino kino "Pobjeda". Odlazeći tamo prisjećala sam se projekcije "Cyranoa" u kinu "Zadar" održane na početku rata pred tri i pol čovjeka u gledalištu (jedan je spavao). Za Zadrane ni daroviti nosonja

Depardieux tada nije bio dovoljno smiješan. Pretpostavljam da su muškarci koji imaju duha i koji požrtvovno i velikodušno, potpisujući tuđe ime, pišu ljubavna pisma već davno izašli iz mode.

A nekidašnji je odlazak u kino predstavljao za me veliku prekretnicu. Dapače, bila je to pomalo bizarna pustolovina. Valjalo se naime usuditi: nakon svih onih studentskih hodočašća u zagrebačka kina poput šarmantnog "Jadrana", intelektualističke "Kinoteke", šminkerskog "Studija" i baroknog "Balkana", koji je prije par godina prekršten u "Europu" (možda zbog one latinske "Nomina sunt odiosa" - "Imena su mrska"). Vrijedilo se usuditi, velim. Jer predvorje "Pobjede", suviše mračno da bi se smatralo osvijetljenim, više je nalik predvorju kuće sumnjiva morala negoli kulturne ustanove tako zvučnoga imena. Slavna bi trebala biti ova građevina! Ta dogodine se ima slaviti stota obljetnica prve javne kino predstave u povijesti kinematografije. Ali, ovo je ratna zona, javio bi se netko. I ovo nije Pariz, znam.

Bio je dugačak red za kartu: "Aladin" i njegova svjetiljka očito su pobudili veliko zanimanje. Odrasli i djeca željni su čarolija. Željni su bajki. (Uostalom, da li bajke još uvijek postoje? I nakon posljednje tri godine?) U onih desetak metara do gospođe koja trga karte na ulazu u dvoranu pomislih da bi kinu trebalo pokloniti koju žarulju kako bi barem put do holywoodske iluzije bio osvijetljen. Film je bio krasan: slike su se izmjenjivale tako brzo da se nisu mogli "pohvatati" svi oni štosevi Disneyjevih učenika. Boje s velikog platna ozarile su velika i mala lica u sjedalima našeg malog (provincijskog?) kina nalik onima iz neorealističnih talijanskih filmova u kojima se u crno-bijeloj tehnici obvezno gega barem jedan mjesni ridikul i nadima barem jedna prsata dama problematične darežljivosti.

Bila je to bajka. Aladin i Jasmina pobijedili su opakog čarobnjaka i vjenčali se. Poslije su valjda imali puno djece pa im se smanjio porez na dohodak. A sve pomoću čarobne svjetiljke i njezina mišićavog duha koji, da sreća bude potpuna, na koncu stječe slobodu. Sve bi bilo dobro da nečiji cinični tata pri izlasku iz kina nije primijetio kako je Aladin - musliman.

Eh, a meni se samo učinilo da bi bilo dobro barem načas prisvojiti onu zahrđalu svjetiljku i zamoliti duha da od našega jedinog kina napravi kuću tek mrvu dostojniju braće Lumiere. Sa samo par dodatnih žarulja i nekoliko kila žute boje za vrata i štokove. Možda bismo "Pobjedom" mogli pobijediti one dosadne i omamljujuće TV i video kutije koji se od kućnih ljubimaca pretvaraju u obiteljske gazde. Ali ovo nije Pariz, znam.

Ipak, možda jednoga dana i dođemo do "Pobjede".

JELE

30. siječnja 1994.
Reinkarnacija

Kad sam jednoga popodneva ušla u dvorište dubrovačkog Interuniverzitetskog centra, Chester Beers, Amerikanac hrvatskoga podrijetla čiju je dob bilo nemoguće odrediti, bio je naslonjen na betonsku ogradu pred ulazom u zgradu. Bio je blijed i teško je disao. Rekao je da je šetajući precijenio svoje tjelesne mogućnosti i do krajnosti se umorio. Zaključivši vjerojatno da sam ja iz nekakve ljubaznosti prešutjela svoja dodatna pitanja, Ches je sam objasnio kako mu je kapacitet pluća veoma malen jer su mu pluća uništena udisanjem otrovnog plina u ratu. Vijetnamskom ratu.

Zapanjenost činjenicom da je čovjek poput krhkoga Beersa sudjelovao u nekakvom ratu, bilo je uokvireno mojom dotadanjom predodžbom o ratu kao kolektivnom zlu koje je ostalo zaboravljeno negdje u prašnjavim ladicama prošlosti i koje je s vremena na vrijeme oživljavalo u knjigama i na filmu. Više od toga o ratu nisam znala. A onda je iskrsnuo taj Ches, Amerikanac nimalo nalik onim trbušastim, preplanulim sunarodnjacima u kariranim hlačama koji na aerodromu strpljivo čuvaju ženin prtljag. Kad se dakle pojavio netko osakaćena tijela, netko tko nije mogao ni hodati ni disati poput drugih ljudi i čija je nemoć bila groteskna u usporedbi s bajkovitošću predjela urešena divovskom procvalom agavom - tek onda je u moje poimanje stvarnosti mogla biti pohranjena predodžba o tomu što uistinu znači i predstavlja - RAT.

"*U kolovozu 1967. Chester Beers postao je stopostotnim invalidom. Roditelji njegove majke bili su podrijetlom Hrvati koji su u Ameriku doselili 1913. godine. Ches je rođen u Californiji, ali je po povratku iz rata živio u Oregonu. Godine 1985. preživio je gotovo fatalnu upalu pluća nakon čega se posvetio pisanju pjesama osjećajući ujedno veliku žudnju za putovanjem. Proputovao je Ameriku, Kanadu i Europu, da bi konačno došao u domovinu svoga djeda, gdje se najdulje zadržao...*" *(iz predgovora zbirke u rukopisu)*

Ches je pisao ode Dubrovniku, Hvaru, Jadranu... Na trenutke mi se činilo da pretjeruje u svom oduševljenju. Ono što je on udisao punim *ostatkom* svojih pluća meni se činilo običnim, svakodnevnim. Pisao je i o svojim ratnim drugovima.

Nakon Dubrovnika sreli smo se još jednom: u Zagrebu. Tada mi je dao rukopis svoje zbirke pjesama. Htio je da ju prevedem. Pa da je možda objave ovdje, u Hrvatskoj. Nakon toga dobila sam još poneko pismo. I razglednicu, s jedrenjacima. Posljednje pismo koje sam primila bilo je moje vlastito na kojem je bio utisnut pečat "Deceased"[12].

U jesen 1991. Interuniverzitetski centar u Dubrovniku pogođen je granatom. Ovdje se naime, Chesteru Beersu, *wherever you are,*[13] u međuvremenu odigrao jedan novi Saigon. I Da Nang. I Hue...[14]

* * *

Groznica je gadna stvar. Ne dopušta da se usredotočiš ni na što. Ležeći u krevetu buljim preko pokrivača kroz nevjerojatno ružičaste zastore i prozorsko staklo oblijepljeno selotejpom (kako se ne bi razletjelo od detonacija!) u rublje što se neumoljivo njiše amo-tamo na balkonskom sušilu. Poput Villonovih obješenih tijela iza prozirne sentimentalnosti.

Pronašao sam ime prijatelja
Kojega sam poznavao u srednjoj školi
Na Crnom Zidu.
A onda sam našao drugo ime.
Potražio sam svoje vlastito
Ali njega tamo nije bilo.[15]

31. siječnja 1994. (*Narodni list*)
"Nakon rata" - u navodnicima

Formalno. Formalno se možemo i rukovati. S osobom koju upravo upoznajemo, s prijateljem ili - s neprijateljem. Onim državnim, mislim. Koji nas je bombardirao, ubijao, silio da životarimo bez struje, vode, bez prometnih veza. A zbog tog istog neprijatelja pomno smo slušali ponoćne vijesti na škrgutavom radiju istrošenih baterija. Zbog toga smo se neprijatelja kočili kad bi tresnula vrata nečijeg automobila. Usred bijela dana koračali smo po zadarskim ulicama čeznuvši za tim da barem taj pseudo-politički (jer o politici nitko ništa ne zna!) razgovor s prijateljem, ta kava, barem tih sljedećih pola sata prođe u miru.

Pa ipak, unatoč svemu tome, mnogi su od nas odlazili na otvaranja izložbi, na promocije knjiga, na koncerte u Donatu. Dok je tutnjalo, dok se rušilo. Dapače, dok se umiralo. Koristili smo svaku prigodu ušutkati

---

[12] "Preminuo" (engl.)
[13] "gdje god bio" (engl.)
[14] "Reinkarnacija" iz naslova ovoga teksta zapravo upućuje na beskrajan niz „reinkarnacija" u tijelima ratnih invalida. Bilo kojega rata.
[15] Beersovi stihovi

nametnuto nam duhovno isposništvo. Forsirali smo život. Ili privid života. Bili smo gordi, gorki, patetični...

No nakon svega toga, "nakon rata" (s navodnicima ili bez njih), uvijek slijedi, razumije se, pokapanje ratne sjekire. Slijedi mir u kojem se doduše pale svijeće za mrtve, ali se i okreću nove stranice, stvaraju planovi, upoznaju ljudi. Rukuje se s ljudima. S prijateljima. Neprijateljima. Formalno. Kao na početku priče. *Kažu da će Ceca (nije li to Arkanova draga?) uskoro održati koncert usred Zagreba.*

Pa ipak, one koji se rukuju s ovim potonjima usrdno molim da me poštede osmjeha "od uha do uha"; Vukovar, Škabrnja i sve ono što još uvijek u Hrvatskoj leži u ruševinama nije posljedica dvorišne tuče uvrijeđenih dječaka. Doista, ostavite mi još toliko hrvatskog ili, točnije, zadarskog dostojanstva da se ne moram - smješkati...

JELE

20. ožujka 1994.

Prije dva dana ušli smo u konfederaciju s Bosnom. Jučer su, čujem, neke granate pale pokraj motela smještena na ulazu u Biograd. Pontonski most učestalo gađaju.

Usprkos tomu Zadar oživljava.

Ipak se bojim. Posljednjih mjeseci: samoće najviše. "Gospodin", kako sam čula, oženio se u prosincu.

9. travnja 1994.

Čini mi se kao da posljednjih mjeseci usamljenost jednostavno zrači iz mene. Iskazuje se kroz smetenost, rastrzanost, umor. Danas sam dobila jedan od prvih primjeraka časopisa *Glasje*. Našega časopisa.

20. prosinca 1994.

Nedavno mi je Davor Ž., koji je prije petnaestak godina napustio Zadar i po svoj će prilici živjeti doživotno u (tuzemnoj ili inozemnoj) dijaspori, rekao sljedeće: "U Zadru nemoj raditi ništa javno. Pusti ih: jednostavno sve što radiš radi za sebe i ne srljaj na vjetrenjače. Svaki posao osim privatnog u Zadru je besmislica."

19. siječnja 1995.

Stiglo je. Jutros. U kuverti boje sladoleda od pistacia. S Elizabetinom glavom u uglu. Pismo. Civilizirano. Gotovo mirisno. Snježanino. Još nije otvoreno. Leži tu, na stolu, od jutros.

* * *

U jesen 1991. fluorescentne boje plakata u londonskoj podzemnoj željeznici izgledale su kao da će se odlijepiti i otpasti sa zida. Novi album irskog kantautora Van Morrisona, Nobelova nagrada za književnost Nadine Gordimer (Južnoafrička Republika), novi film pod naslovom *Object of Beauty* (u glavnoj ulozi John Malkovich, a Glen Close u filmu nekog banalnog naslova)... Slijedi plakat sa šokantnim pitanjem: "How is it to be raped at the age of 3?"[16] Nižu se ležernost, neopterećenost, (lažna) sućut, zapadnjačka sentimentalnost...

Koje to milje dijele tebe od mene, mene od tebe, Snježana? Milje prostora? Milje iskustva?

* * *

Pismo je do danas ostalo neotvoreno. Leži vjerojatno u nekoj ladici. Mislim da će tako i ostati. Snježana, *sorry*, nemaš mi što reći. Kao ni ja tebi.

Nothing of importance. Ništa važno.

* * *

Gospode, htjela bih živjeti drukčije. Previše ljudi vjeruje kako bi ostali trebali živjeti po njihovim pravilima. Hvatam posljednje čestice danjeg svjetla. Nisam u stanju više s Matovilkom pjevati "Moja domovina". Glas neće iz grla.

20. siječnja 1995.

Syndrom Iadertinum (*Narodni list*)

Čini se da se Zadrani teško odlučuju poslati svoj glas izvan granica grada. Razlozi su zacijelo političke naravi u što samo rijetki mogu i žele zalaziti.

Obično tako Zadrani prepuštaju drugima da uobliče predodžbu o životu u njihovu gradu. Tijekom proteklih (ratnih) godina trominutni zapisi u TV-dnevniku uglavnom su se svodili na konstataciju o broju ranjenih ili poginulih. (Živi i preživjeli nisu bili bog-zna-kako medijski zanimljivi.) Povremeno bi se na televiziji pojavio kakav dokumentarac - poput "Zlatnog i srebrnog Zadra" (financiran iz zadarskih izvora) autor kojega ovdje će biti naznačen tek sa "Nomina sunt odiosa" - nudeći na fragmentaran i, rekla bih, površan način "pravu sliku" o onome što se u Zadru zbivalo ovih godina. Kuriozitet vezan za spomenuti film jest činjenica da je za potrebe njegova snimanja na zadarskom Poluotoku par

---

[16] "Kako je to biti silovan u dobi od tri godine?" (engl.)

sati bila isključena struja kako bi se mogli snimiti "upečatljivi" *chiaro-scuro* prizori s licima nad svijećama, nalik na ona s platna Michelangela Caravaggia. Od emitiranja toga filma pitam se gdje su bili snimatelji dok ovdje mjesecima neprekidno nije bilo struje. (Možda i zato simbola Zadra neće biti na novim novčanicama. Slika agregata neprimjerena je jer budi ružne uspomene.)

Kako "šlag na torti" zna biti gorak potvrdila je nedavna posjeta Zadru jednog Intelektualca, veoma "rasprostranjene" (u funkcionalnom smislu) osobe s HRT-a, povodom mogućeg ponovnog otvaranja televizijskog studija u ovom gradu. Na tiskovnoj konferenciji Intelektualac je iznio svoj stav o Zadru, Zadranima, zadarskim novinarima, sportašima, pedagozima (dakle o mnogočemu, kako već dolikuje koleričnom *uomo universaleu* koji se, čini se, obrazovan i odgajan po ubrzanoj "metodi stripa", dohvatio politike pa sad njome šiba na sve strane teatralno "istresajući" svoj sud i gdje treba i gdje ne treba.) Reći za riječi gospodina s HRT-a da predstavljaju uvrede i blaćenje zadarske ratne i poratne svakodnevnice - puki je eufemizam. Nazvati ih pak poniženjem opet nije dobar izbor riječi s obzirom da je tom poniženju prethodilo ono koje je trajalo svih ovih ratnih godina, a koje se službeno zove "opća opasnost".

Ali: svako čudo za tri dana. "Ekcesne situacije" voda brzo odnese i od logički i psihološki opravdanog protesta ostanu tek žalopoljke koje se na Narodnom trgu, u podnevnim čakulama, prežvakavaju kao kakav digestiv prije objeda, u krugovima znanaca, s rukama u džepovima - i ništa.

Ovakvo se ponašanje može promatraču izvana doimati zanimljivim pa ga možda netko za par godina u medicinskim leksikonima zabilježi kao "Zadarski sindrom" (Syndrom Iadertinum). A taj se pučki može obrazložiti ovako: ako te netko pljune, okreni mu spremno drugi obraz. Za drugo pljuvanje.

JELE

12. veljače 1995.

Jutros oko četiri na glavnoj je tržnici eksplodirala, kažu, mina montirana pod jednim kioskom. U trenutku ekspozije u blizini kioska nalazio se policajac koji je teško ranjen. Ovu vijest Jasenka, s kojom sam večeras bila u kinu, nije mi htjela reći sve do trena kad smo nakon odgledanog (odličnog) filma *Forrest Gump* otišle u "Mozaik" na piće.

Ovo je samo jedan od sličnih događaja koji su se posljednih mjeseci zbili u Zadru. Nešto prije Božića u Tehničkoj školi, tijekom velikoga odmora, odletio je u zrak jedan učenik čije su komadiće tijela nalazili kasnije kilometar od zgrade u kojoj se eksplozija dogodila.

A mi, koji ostajemo nakon ovih događaja, sve smo tuplji spram nasilnoj ili samoubilačkoj smrti, koja u nas postaje svakodnevnicom. Kad sve ovo završi nipošto neću imati vremena za svoje gluposti i tuđe svinjarije.

7. travnja 1995.

Danas smo imali prigodu vidjeti praizvedbu komada *Zvjezdan* u izvedbi glumaca zadarskoga Kazališta lutaka. Komad je temeljen na dramatizaciji pripovijetke engleskoga pisca larpurlartista Oscara Wildea, s početka ovoga stoljeća. Riječ je o priči o dobru i zlu koji se poput jina i janga izmjenjuju. Gospođa Dundov uspješno je iskoristila predložak koji je dobar primjer Wildeove paradokalne i goteskne literature. Dječaka Zvjezdana, kojega jedne zvjezdane noći u šumi pronalazi šumar i odgaja u svojoj siromašnoj, ali već mnogobrojnoj obitelji. Zvjezdan međutim usprkos plemenitosti i dobroti ljudi kojima je okružen predstavlja oličenje zla; on širi zlo gdjegod stigne pa i kad sreće svoju pravu, ostarjelu i siromašnu majku. Zbog svoje je opakosti kažnjen time da se od prelijepog zlatokosog dječaka pretvara u rugobu koja nigdje nije dobrodošla, koju tjeraju i muče. No, Zvjezdan od zloga kralja dobiva zadaću pronaći zlato. Unatoč mukotrpnosti zadaće on zlato pronalazi, ali ga daruje prosjaku. Nakon brojnih nevolja Zvjezdan je – kao u pravoj bajci - nagrađen: vraćen mu je prijašnji lijepi lik, zbog stečene plemenitosti postaje vladar kraljevstva a na koncu priče doznaje da su majka i prosjak njegovi roditelji. Lutke u ovoj predstavi podsjećaju na one poljskog kazališta animacije iz Jelenie Góre, koji je na prošlogodišnjem PIF-u prikazao predstavu *Ormar* temeljenu na poemi Guillaumea Apollinairea i bajci *Postojani kositreni vojnik* Hansa Christiana Andersena.

U takodjer Wildeovu *Dorianu Grayju*, prisjećam se, središnji lik izjavljuje kako misli da je bolje biti lijep negoli dobar. Razmišljam o dvojnosti iste osobe, o ljepoti viđenoj kao fizička manifestacija zla i ružnoći kao odrazu dobrote i plemenitosti, ili pak o ružnoći kao kazni za počinjene grijehe, o Wildeovu esteticizmu engleske secesije…

Razmišljam o dobru i zlu utjelovljenima u istoj osobi, fasciniranosti ljepotom koja može biti tek krinka zla i okrutnosti, o esteticizmu u kojem se traga za dobrim. Čudovišnost zakrabuljena ili zaogrnuta ljepotom, čudovišnost koja poprima svoje pravo obličje u nakaznosti i odvratnosti. Traganje za dobrim i lijepim u istoj spodobi.

Je li *Zvjezdan* bajka za odrasle? Bajke su, kažu, didaktična literatura koja djecu uči da postoji dobro i zlo, lijepo i nakazno, jin i jang, apstraktna duhovna iskvarenost, grijeh preobražen ljepotom. Porok i vrlina ovdje su građa za umjetničko djelo.

Treba li nam u ovom trenutku bajka da bismo povjerovali u postojanje dobra?

27. travnja. 1995.
Odvezla se u Biograd. Umalo da nisam razbila tatin auto prelazeći u okuci pred nadolazećim autom. Škare. Mamin povratak s pregleda u Zagrebu: blaga kolagenoza.

5. svibnja 1995.
Sa studentima i glumcima zadarskoga Kazališta lutaka (*Zlatko, Dragan, Anđela - biseri hrvatskog lutkarstva...*) radim u malom kazalištu u Jazinama na scenskom kolažu pod naslovom *Kolega, rat predugo traje....* kojega temeljim na dramatizaciji vlastitih tekstova, objavljenih u *Narodnom listu* tijekom 1992. i 1993. pod pseudonimom "Jele" te na nekolicini tekstova čitanih u radio-emisiji *Usprkos*. Prije nekoliko dana, u granatiranju Zagreba, ranjen je mladić Luka Skračić, daroviti student režije. Pitanje je hoće li Luka preživjeti. (*"Ponekad mi se čini da ću od bola izgubiti razum", reče mi nedugo nakon što se ono dogodilo kolega Vlado, otac pokojnoga Luke, prelazeći sa mnom zadarski Most.*) Među studentima s kojima radim na predstavi ima njegovih rođaka. *Rat doista predugo traje...*

20. svibnja 1995. (*Narodni list*)
- - - Čini se da se Zadrani teško odlučuju poslati svoj glas izvan granica grada. Razlozi su zacijelo političke naravi, u što samo rijetki mogu i žele zalaziti.

Obično tako Zadrani prepuštaju drugima da uobliče predodžbu o životu u njihovu gradu. Tijekom proteklih (ratnih) godina trominutni zapisi u TV-dnevniku uglavnom su se svodili na konstataciju o broju ranjenih ili poginulih. Živi i preživjeli nisu (bili) bog-zna-kako medijski zanimljivi. Možda i zato simbola Zadra neće biti na novim novčanicama. Slika agregata neprimjerena je jer budi ružne uspomene. - - -

JELE

28. srpnja 1995.
Svrha od teatra (*Narodni list*)
Svaka čast, Davore! Tako bi vjerojatno svi koji poznaju Davora Žagara, redatelja i adaptatora Kušanova kazališnog komada *Svrha od slobode*, trebali s poštovanjem kazati nakon odgledane predstave.

Preplavljeni dojmovima neposredno nakon odgledane predstave temeljene na Kušanovu dramskom tekstu *Svrha od slobode* teško da ćemo znati što kazati. Dajući presjek povijesti "slobodnoga" grada, povijesti koja se rasprodaje (jer je povijest - sudbina), Licitator u lucifersko-šerbedžijinskoj maniri odbrojava: Prvi put...drugi put... A svaka nova licitacija, i svaka nova prodaja zapravo je ponovno proživljavanje istovjetnog ciklusa vlastite Povijesti od koje se ne uči ništa, dapače - koju se ušutkuje. Porfirogenet, vođa Gusara, Venecijanaca, Francuza ili pak Ferdinand - tek je podla/ nasilna/ shizofrena/ jalova/ degenerična itd. varijanta na temu vladara - koju bravurozno (re)inkarnira Slavko Juraga. Gundulićevo “Kolo sreće uokoli... “ dobija u Žagarovoj adaptaciji završnicu: tko bi doli, dol (i) ostaje. Sad je to “Kolo sreće” Tanje Tušek, na kojemu su među zgodicima: Francuzi, Mleci, Turci, Austrijanci ili pak sladoled, burek (sa srdelama)...možda i čevapčići. Ali kako god "okreneš" ne gine ti tuđa vlast.

A kad se konačno javi Gracij(el)a, djeva kojoj tijekom predstave kao kakvom Diogenu ili liku iz *Božanstvene komedije* kojemu iz blata tek glava proviruje, pojavljuje a koja je svoje djevičanstvo čuvala za Franu, a izgubila ga s Turkom, ima nade jer će ona svoje djevičanstvo ponovno doseći na izvoru Zrmanje. To je naime Žaragovo predviđanje sudbine one kojoj danas pjevaju (prve) pjesme, zbog koje su sjedili u zatvorima, koju žele rasprodati. U ratu? Nego što, a kad ćeš nego u ratu. (Rasprodaja, a onda pretvorba - da poslije ne bi bilo: nismo znali).

Zacijelo bi svako novo čitanje ponudilo novo značenje ove predstave. Žagar je okupio mladi ansambl Glumačkoga studija i pokrenuo sve njihove potencijale, oslobodio ih je do vriska, smijeha, pjesme. Mislim, da bismo mu na tome trebali biti zahvalni.

28. kolovoza 1995.

Maločas sam na televiziji vidjela slike prijepodnevnog pokolja na sarajevskoj tržnici. Rekli su da je tamo oko 11 sati pala granata i da je pobijeno trideset dvoje ljudi, uglavnom djece, žena i staraca. Mislim da u ovih četiri ili pet godina otkako traje (n)ova balkanska klaonica nisam naučila gledati na sve te smrti kao na kolektivnu brojku gdje tragedija pojedinca nije bitna. Ništa ja nisam naučila.

Jutros sam nakon pune četiri godine čula glas Tanje A., moje negdanje srednjoškolske kolegice, studentske prijateljice i cimerice kod gazdarice u Gajevoj. Došla je iz Slovenije, kući na ljetovanje. Htjela je da se nađemo. Nakon četiri godine šutnje. Da idemo nekamo zajedno na kupanje. Nakon četiri godine šutnje. Njezina nejavljanja. Nepitanja što je s mojim djetetom, je li živo, zdravo, je li preživjelo ovaj užas. Nisam pristala. Dijalog je bio kratak i završio mojim britkim: "Dobro Tanja, bog!". Drukčije nisam ni mogla reći.

Inače, momak koji je nestao u vidu "mesne" prašine u Tehničkoj školi prošloga Božića – mislim da je njezin nećak. Sjećam ga se kao sasvim malog dječaka. Imao je ime. Znakovito. Neven.

3. travnja 1996.
U avionskoj nesreći u Konavlima poginuo Nikša Antonini, moj prijatelj.

Na Uskrs, 1996.
Netom protekli blagdan bio je zacijelo najtužniji Uskrs slavljen u našem domu. Iako smo mu se nakon prethodnih pet ratnih i tjeskobnih trebali posebno radovati.

Planirana krigla najboljega belgijskog piva ostala je neispijena...

Novinska fotografija prepolovljenog aviona u brdima ponad Konavala nema pandana u riječima. Fotografi su u prednosti: nad nesrećom se ne moraju truditi izgovarati - riječi.

Ono Nikšino: "A kako van je doli?" - koje bi za ratnih dana doprlo iz telefonske slušalice - sada poprima jedno sasma neočekivano značenje...

9. travnja 1996.
Kad bih mogla zahvatiti i u sebe primiti barem dio Tinine boli! [17]
Postoji li kakav kirurški postupak kojim bi se to izvelo?

17. travnja 1996.
Predstavljanje *Pogleda* u prostoru Društva hrvatskih književnika u Zagrebu.

U predstavljanju sudjelovali Petar Marija Radelj - fratar dominikanac, Ante Stamać - predsjednik DHK, kritičar Božidar Petrač i dramski umjetnik Zlatko Crnković. Bio je tamo i Pavle. *Za moje bližnje - Petra i Pavla - ovo nešto vrijedi. Ima li još koji svetac na mojoj strani?*

30. travnja 1996.
Travanj je najokrutniji mjesec, što rađa
Jorgovane iz mrtve zemlje, i miješa
Sjećanje i želju.[18]

3. kolovoza 1996.
Silvana je otišla. Svojevoljno. U 44. godini. Moji razgovori s njom o besmislenosti njezina braka postali su također besmisleni. Iz jednjaka mi u

---

[17] Tina je bila Nikšina žena i moja prijateljica.
[18] Iz *Puste zemlje* T. S. Eliota.

usta mili metalan okus. *Još mi i danas, nakon toliko godina, u mislima odzvanja njezin smijeh iz prekrasnih punih usana.*

29. kolovoza 1996.
(ulomak iz kazališnog osvrta objavljenog u *Vijencu*)
Organizatori zadorskog Kazališnog ljeta na prvim su konferencijama za novinstvo tvrdili da je najveći događaj Ljeta Goldonijeva *Kafeterija*. Danas pak tvrde da je to *Pjesnička kob*. Zbunjujuće. Nejasnoće u ovoj priči (koje se nekima mogu činiti nevažnim formalnostima) ipak navode na zaključak da bi bilo lijepo kada bi dva i dva bili – pet. Šteta. Jer, u cjelini uzevši, zadarska kazališna ljeta mnogo dobra nude Zadru i njegovim građanima. Ili, kako reče predsjednik upravnog vijeća Hrvatske kazališne kuće u Zadru: "Zadar je prepoznao kazališe, kazalište je prepoznalo Zadar". Što je mnogo važnije od profita pojedinaca. Pa ako pojedinci i uzimaju slobodu i moć provoditi vlastite projekte kroz poslove HKK, nije jasno zašto se mora čekati npr. kongres hrvatskih liječnika potkraj rujna tj. početkom jeseni da bi se istodobno na otvorenom na relativno niskoj temperaturi održala jedna "ljetna" kazališna premijera. Ili su i godišnja doba postala predmetom manipulacije povlaštenih persona? Ostaje nam da za neke odgovore pričekamo jesen… I opet uz geslo ovogodišnjeg Kazališnog ljeta: "Poštenje i čast najvažniji su čoviku. A u Zadru duplo!"

21. rujna 1996.
Uđem polako u Sv. Stošiju. Velika je i prazna. Ugodno je obaviti se samoćom, tišinom i nevidljivim lebdećim dušama u prostoru katedrale, pa se prepustiti nostalgičnim sjećanjima na nama drage, kojih više nema.

15. listopada 1996.
Ima nešto u mirisu prve polovice listopada kada se nosnice šire pred oštrim, kao mentom začinjenim zrakom između dva pljuska u osunčanu krugu nimalo toplijem od hladovine. Miris izvlači iz sjećanja duše onih koji nas upućuju na ono što može a ne mora biti.

3. siječnja 1997.
Godina žene (nikad objavljeni članak)
Prije tridesetak godina u autobiografskom romanu *Stakleno zvono* američka spisateljica i pjesnikinja Sylvia Plath napisala je sljedeće:
"Također sam pamtila da je Buddy Willard rekao na neki zloslutan, znalački način da ću se drukčije osjećati kada dobijem djecu, da više neću željeti pisati pjesme. Tako sam počela misliti kako je, možda, točno da

brak i djeca djeluju kao da ti je mozak ispran te da poslije tupo ideš naokolo kao rob u nekoj privatnoj totalitarnoj državi..."

Netom nakon objavljivanja ovoga romana Sylvia je prestala pisati pjesme. Bila je udata, bila je majka, ali je njezin tko-zna-koji pokušaj samoubojstva konačno uspio.

Nakon ovoga turobnog početka napomenut ću da ovo nije članak o feminizmu (koji mi je osobno nedrag zato što je, vjerujem, sam po sebi potvrda diskriminacije u oba smjera, pa i zato što se njime kao porugom i etiketom služe muškarci koji u raspravi nemaju "boljega argumenta"); ovdje će naime biti riječi o nekim ženama koje uporno nastoje pisati/pjevati pjesme.

* * *

Za ilustraciju su mi potrebne sljedeće dvije priče. Prva priča: kad je Annie Mae Bullock poznatija pod imenom Tina Turner raskinula sa svojim ovisničkim životom krotke pratilje supruga Ikea, mnogi su pomislili da je tobože slabija (čitaj: lošija) polovica bračnog para Ike & Tina zauvijek izgubljena u labirintu anonimnosti. Danas, u šestom desetljeću života, "tigrica", tako kažu, uživa u slobodi izvan bračnog i stvaralačkog kalupa priređujući koncerte za čitave stadione obožavatelja. Druga priča: jedna druga "tigrica" svojem je menedžeru tijekom prijema u svađi bacila u lice hrpu ruža. Kad ju je na to ovaj u bijesu polio šampanjcem, ona je šampanjac iz vlastite čaše izlila sebi na glavu želeći time pokazati da joj nitko ne može učiniti ono što ona sama ne može učiniti sebi. Bila je to Bette Midler a spomenuti prijem održan je prigodom promocije kultnog filma "Ruža" u kojem Bette portretira Rose, pjevačku zvijezdu nesposobnu da se suprotstavi agresivnom i manipulirajućem menedžeru. Ali, Bette očito nije Rose...

Tina i Bette nisu pjesnikinje u klasičnom smislu riječi, ali zato predstavljaju velika imena rock/pop scene u kojoj pjevači(ce) nisu tek puke interpretatorice tuđe glazbe i stihova, već nude vlastite tekstove a time i vlastitu osobnost. U proteklih dvadesetak godina uz bok Tini i Bette stajale su/stoje "tigrice" poput Debbie Harry - Blondie, Chrissie Hynde, Cyndi Lauper, Madonne... Vjerojatno bi se taj sve veći utjecaj žena na sceni mogao dovesti u vezu s poplavom stilova i ritmova kojom je označeno rečeno razdoblje. Kažu da su u svakoj modi prvi i posljednji pobornici smiješni. Usredotočimo li se na glazbu osamdesetih godina i primijenimo li spomenutu izreku na rock i pop glazbu upravo tih godina, moglo bi se zaključiti da se u tom desetljeću izmjenjivanje stilova, lica i trendova odvijalo takvom silovitom brzinom da se nikada nije znalo tko će ispasti smiješan. Usprkos sve izraženijoj globalnoj gospodarskoj stagnaciji te rastućem broju nezaposlenih mladih ljudi, osamdesetih se godina želja mladeži za provodom kao i njihova lakomislena vedrina i žar - nisu gasili. Naprotiv, čini se kao da je raspad ekonomskog ustroja bio pogodnom pozornicom još žešćeg rasplamsavanja pohlepe za glazbenim užitkom. To je navelo jednog rock kritičara da mladež osamdetih usporedi s bendom koji svira i putnicima koji plešu na tonućem Titanicu.

Doba je to glazbenog šarenila: antologijskih uzdaha zanesenog i (voajerski) zanosnog potčinjavanja partneru jedne Jane Birkin, francuske pjevačice i glumice čija pjesma "Je t'aime" zvuči tako - francuski, romantično pa i "nevino" u usporedbi s orgazmičkom, elektronskom mješavinom uzdaha i metronomskog disco ritma Donne Summer i drugih "kompjutorskih" izvođača iz osamdesetih koja se često svodila na ironičan dokument o ženskoj spolnosti. Ili još pogubnije: o spolnoj samodostatnosti.

Poruke spomenutih vampova rock/pop scene osamdesetih temeljile su se uglavnom na seksualnosti i agresivnosti, dakle na onome što je dotad po redu stvari bilo zabranjeno voće za mazohizmom i samozatajnošću obilježen spol. Medena nevinost Olivije Newton John, ženstvena bezopasnost lahoraste Kate Bush ili elegancija pjevačke Nefertiti - Sade Adu, još su i te kako značajne, ali osobine njihova izraza po svemu sudeći ne mogu privući čitave stadione ljudi kao što to mogu "tigrice" s početka teksta. Uostalom, ni u književnosti likovi koji su "kreposni" nemaju potencijal koji bi od njih načinio prave junake. Ti su likovi odveć neutralni, pa i dosadni da bi postali "legendama".

Opirući se prosječnosti, podređenosti i ustaljenoj predodžbi žene grešnice/patnice - nove Ivane Orleanske rock umjetnosti spašavaju domovinu iskrenosti iako konačno uglavnom završavaju na lomači erosa, srdžbe i osvetoljublja. Izrazita senzualnost ženskih ekstrovertiranih introvertita (ili onih s obrnutom kombinacijom) nije lagodna osobina jer izaziva prkos i neprijateljstvo "jačega" spola. Ženino obasipanje osjećajima, nuđenje "srca na dlanu" - što se povremeno shvaća kao svojevrsno prostituiranje - često nailazi na izluđujuću ravnodušnost muškarca kojemu je primjerenjiji čir na želucu od suznih ispovijedanja. ON, navikao na netom pripravljen objed i čisto rublje, nipošto ne želi zalaziti u složeni mehanizam ženskih osjećaja. Barem ne kod vlastite žene.

Vezano za tu ne osobito udobnu i ugodnu stranu ženske osjećajnosti britanska pjevačica Alison Moyet kazala je jednom prigodom kako joj se sviđa stil pjevanja crnih pjevačica jer su one spremne izraziti one manje lijepe osobine žene: posesivnost, ljubomoru i beskrupuloznost. Alisonina pjesma "All Cried Out" predstavlja pravu himnu raskidanja sa ženskom ovisnošću i plitkom podređenošću kojom se zauzvrat stvara privid neusamljenosti jer je muškarac tjelesno (ali samo tjelesno) nazočan.

Međutim, spomenuto, zabranjeno voće slobodnoga izjašnjavanja nije jednostavno doseći. Da bi mogle iskazati sve svoje skrivene ili potiskivane tabu poruke pjevačice obično pribjegavaju raznim sredstvima koja ih barem prividno izjednačuju ili približavaju muškarcima. Neke se tako, poput Annie Lenox ili Sinead O'Connor, odlučuju na androgin image žene koja izgledom kao da "depersonalizira muškarca koji depersonalizira ženu"... Druge pak, koje ne pristaju na izgled dvospolca kose ošišane "ne četku", na muška odijela ili trikoom spljoštena prsa ostaju ženstvene izgledom ali tek zato jer su obdarene "zahvalnim" hrapavim glasom nalik onom Roda Stewarta. Takvu sirovu senzualnost u glasu posjeduju Elkie Brooks, Bonnie Tyler, Joan Armatrading i velika glumačko-pjevačka zvijezda Cher.

Postoji i ona skupina pjevačica koje, u nemogućnosti da se pohvale vanjštinom, gaje ponekad izgled nonšalantne pa i pomalo neuredne vještice koja uvijek ima nešto reći. Gianna Nannini, temperamentna talijanska kantautorica, u nas poznatija tek po izvođenju Mundialove nogometne himne, može sebi priuštiti prosječan izgled prodavačice s Ponterossa samo zato što je glazbeno izuzetno nadarena. Na nastupima Nannini djeluje muškobanjasto, a svoju aroganciju sažima u jednoj pjesmi poručujući svome dragome: "Chi sa chi vincerà?" (Tko zna tko će pobijediti?) Unatoč svom energičnom i nimalo ženstvenom stilu, Gianna Nannini ima danas klubove obožavatelja po čitavoj Zapadnoj Europi.

Četvrta skupina ženskih izvođača odabrala je jarko narumenjene usne, široki osmijeh bisernih zubiju i, dakako, oksidiranu kosa boje izblijedjelog maslačka - izgled možda i stoljetnog estradnog arhetipa utjelovljenog u Marilyn Monroe koji je oživljavao u liku Debbie Harry, Kim Wilde, Anne Oxa, Annie Lennox te konačno, u liku megazvijezde Madonne o kojoj prva rečenica u rock-enciklopediji Mikea Clifforda glasi:"Ponekad je imidž veći od glazbe". U nas pjevačice toga tipa izvirale su kao već zaboravljena "kompjuterska" Marina Perazić, zadarsko-eurovizijska Taichee, izuzetnim glasom obdarena Vanna te mnogo maznija. platinasta verzija Kasandre. Pa ipak, čini se da je danas iza osmišljenog imagea nužno posjedovati i ogromnu količinu talenta.

U okviru ovoga *booma* ženske afirmacije u rock-glazbi i opovrgavanja uvriježenog vjerovanja da su žene u rocku izvođači drugoga reda - pitanje je kako funkcioniraju naše "tigrice", a njih izgleda ipak ima. Naime, uz izuzetne ali ne i komercijalne glasove Josipe Lisac i Zorice Kondže posljednjih su se godina javljaju provokativne, crnokose i prirodne I-Bee sa "šumicom" i "davanjima", kao i Alka koja pristaje na "laganje". Sve izraženije okretanje kolijevci, obitelji kao jezgri društva i ostalim ilirsko-romantičnim modelima osim što je vremenski prevladano u našim se uvjetima doima sve više paradoksalnim. Možda "life stile" sentimentalnih Amerikanaca takve modele i dopušta jer su oni prije svega temeljeni na visokom standardu i ostalim preduvjetima koji nisu skopčani s uznemirenošću i neizvjesnosti kakvima su popraćena politička i društvena previranja u nas. Tko zna koje po redu buđenje nacije spojeno s neprestanom prijetnjom ratom suočeno je na žalost svih nas s masovnom frustracijom i muškog i ženskog dijela stanovništva u kojem nezaustavljivo raste broj socijalnih slučajeva, ljudi s bocom u džepu, broj premlaćenih žena i nezbrinute djece. Svemogući naš *pater familias* svoju ulogu snadbjevača obitelji doživljava sve više promašenom. U istom kruhoborstvu žena, usprkos vraćanju klasičnim poimanjima, ne dobija nikakve povlastice. Dapače, u prividu emancipiranosti, od žene se i dalje očekuje da privređuje za razliku od tobože ne-emancipirane, bezbrižne, debele američke supruge i majke koja djeci za ručak kupuje hamburgere i pizzu.

Prisjećam se stihova Chrissie Hynde. "She wants to be a good mother/so she'll do the best she can/ but what about the other/what about the man?" (Ona želi biti dobra majka, stoga čini najbolje što može/ ali što je s onim drugim, što je s muškarcem?)

S obzirom na okolnosti, usuđujem se predvidjeti da muškarcu našem svagdanjem neće ubuduće biti na sceni potrebna ljutita, agresivna i muškobanjasta ženska spodoba. On će vjerojatno tražiti privid žene koja neće biti oskvrnuta našom svakodnevnicom. Trebat će mu Botticellijeva ljepotica umotana u pastelne, djevičanske velove nespojive sa stečajevima, pretvorbama poduzeća i međunacionalnim sukobima. Uostalom, zašto bi na sceni tražio tigricu ili vješticu kad je već ima kod kuće?

Ali, možda bi se žene sa svojim muškarcima ipak trebale nekako nagoditi. Sjetimo li se Sylvie Plath s početka ovog teksta očekivat ćemo od "slabijeg" spola da usklikne: DOPUSTITE NAM DA I DALJE PIŠEMO PJESME!

À propos pjesama, dadu li se one ilustrirati sljedećim stihovima?

(Kasandra:) Deset puta da je duža noć/ sa mnom biti bilo premalo...

(Alka:) Jašeš kao Johny Wayne/ ove noći tvoj je čitav svijet...

(I Bee:) No-ćno ku-pa-nje, ja ću s tebe papat sol…

A kad je već o soli riječ, pretpostavljam da se za odnose između spolova više neće moći kazati kako su – bljutavi!

5. siječnja 1997.

Za popriličan broj Zadrana 1997. započela je među ostalim i "novogodišnjim balom" (tako su ga najavljivali!) - mješavinom socrealističke predvidljivosti i beskrupuloznosti prvoga stupnja kapitalizma, u dvorani hotela "Novi park". To je bila jedna od prvih proslava nakon rata u spomenutom hotelu; donedavno su tu stanovali prognanici. Nakon što smo uredno uplatili određenu sumu novca *per capita* za nešto što nam se događa jednom u godini, dočekala nas je - lagano, prigodno, slavljenički odjevene nepregledna (čitaj: stol iza stupa!) prostorija bez grijanja, razglas koji je crkao minutu i trideset sekundi nakon što je počela svirka, plesači koji su padali po podiju skliskom zato što je strop prokišnjavao, konobari koji su nam - zbunjeni poslijeratnim stampedom gostiju i naviknuti na prognaničke uzuse - točili skupocjeno vino u čaše u kakvima se u tom istom hotelu po kupaonicama drži četkica za zube... Bila je to potvrda kvalitetne pripremljenosti ovoga "kraja" svijeta za predstojeću turističku sezonu.

8. siječnja 1997.

Dragi striče Vlasto[19],

vjerojatno ćete se veoma iznenaditi ovom pismu. Toliko puta sam ga započinjala pisati (a nekoliko pisama već sam u mislima i dovršila).

Više se ni ne sjećam kad smo se posljednji puta vidjeli. Toliki je vremenski jaz među nama da mi je prilično teško pisati. Od našega zadnjeg viđenja štošta se dogodilo, što me je odvuklo - u čisto instinktivnoj borbi za opstanak - od mnogih (ranijih) kontakata. Razdoblje od 1991. naovamo pretvorilo mi se u svojevrsnu kašu u kojoj je pojedine događaje vrlo teško izdvojiti i sagledati izolirano.

U jesen 1991. počeo je rat a time i vjerojatno najteže razdoblje u mome životu (pod uvjetom da rat ponovno ne doživim!). Mojoj kćeri Emi bilo je godinu i sedam mjeseci kad se ovdje počelo pucati i granatirati. U samom je gradu i među civilima priličan broj ljudi poginuo i bilo je najteže iz trena u tren živjeti s mislima da postoji vrlo velika mogućnost da se mome djetetu nešto strašno dogodi.

---

[19] Pismo je upućeno tatinom rođaku, Vlastimiru (Vlasti) Peričiću, profesoru kompozicije na beogradskoj Muzičkoj akademiji. Njegov otac, Jure, brat mojega djeda, otišao je na studij povijesti i zemljopisa (koji se tada nije mogao studirati u Zagrebu!) u Beograd. Oženivši se profesoricom u ono doba nazivanog „srpsko-hrvatskog" jezika, Jelicom (po kojoj sam trebala dobiti ime Jelena), više se nije vratio u Hrvatsku. Gornje pismo ujedno je jedino koje sam u posljednjih desetak godina odaslala u Srbiju.

U jesen 1992. godine S. i ja smo se na moje inzistiranje razveli (odvojeno smo živjeli već dulje vrijeme i naša je rastava bila logična posljedica svega što je tomu prethodilo). Rat, rastava, malo dijete, nestašica vode, struje, hrane ... ne moram duljiti - bilo je strašno, ali nadam se da je sada gotovo. Makar, sada izviru neki novi problemi: ako se rat može prikazati crnom bojom, onda je poraće itekako natopljeno sivom.

Zbunjuje me to što o tome kako živite ne znam ništa. Kad god Vas se sjetim pomislim kako je gotovo bizarno što se ne čujemo i ne vidimo u ovako teškim okolnostima. Pitala bih povremeno tatu zna li što je s Vama, ali obično bih dobila vrlo neodređene odgovore.

Jeste li razmišljali o tome da dođete malo k nama?

Moram priznati da se s tatom i mamom relativno rijetko vidim i čujem. Unazad par godina (valjda je na to utjecao rat, rastava, različiti pogledi na obiteljske odnose i štošta drugo) nekako smo se udaljili. Ili je možda ona obiteljska prisnost koju je tata nastojao održati bila u bitnim stvarima iluzorna. Teško se i preteško nosim s isključivostima i patrijarhalnim pogledima u našoj obitelji i dolazim do zaključka da je veliki duhovni zločin nekome omogućiti školovanje i intelektualni napredak da bi ga se i u tridesetpetoj prisiljavalo živjeti u "mediteranskim ladicama" u kojima muško-ženski odnosi poprimaju monstruozne razmjere. No, neću Vam dulje o tome dosađivati.

Zaista bih voljela znati što je s Vama, kakvo Vam je zdravlje i treba li Vam štogod.[20] Ova vremenska praznina među nama je, kako rekoh, preduga. No vjerujem da nije i nepremostiva. Javite se.

Voli Vas i srdačno pozdravlja

Helena

21. siječnja 1997.

Jedini zadarski prostor koji mi staloženošću i redom vraća vjeru u obaviještenost i disciplinu jest Znanstvena knjižnica. Zbog visoke kakvoće rada u ratu i poraću dobili su 1995. nagradu Grada Zadra. Veoma zasluženo. Bacam pogled na studente zadubljene u knjigu u suncem okupanoj čitaonici. Duhovna radoznalost, otvorenost prema novim

---

[20] U vrijeme redigiranja ulomaka ovih zapisa u svrhu tiskanja u jednom zagrebackom časopisu, Beograd, mjesto boravka strica Vlaste, dobio je nadimak - Bombaj. Vlastimir Peričić bio je skladatelj, umjetnik, zvjezdoznanac, poliglot, vrhunski intelektualac (završen konzervatorij u Beču), humanist, erudit, pacifist… Stanovao je u to doba na najvišem katu zgrade u Vasinoj, u središtu grada. Kako je do tada dosegao stopostotnu invalidnost - bio je nepokretan - kretao se u kolicima. Ono bez čega u životu nipošto nije mogao bile su - cigarete...

spoznajama, a k tome i ogromna količina tolerancije, velikodušja, altruizma...- klija li bit intelektualnosti na ovakvim mjestima?

23. siječnja 1997.

Obrana disertacije na Filozofskom fakultetu u Zadru. U ocjenjivačkom povjerenstvu dr. Košutić-Brozović, dr. Beker i dr. Mardešić. Profesora Bekera, mog negdanjeg mentora, posljednji sam puta vidjela na postdiplomskom. Nakon ručka otputovao je u Zagreb. Melankolična pitalica: hoće li opet proći desetak godina do našega ponovnog susreta?

Moja disertacija "Posrednici engleske književnosti u hrvatskoj književnoj kritici u razdoblju 1914.-1940." temeljena je na istraživanju bibliografija kritike, prijevoda i kazališnog repertoara iz rečenog perioda, koje sam sama izradila. Središnji dio ove disertacije o recepciji engleske književnosti čini deset monografija o najistaknutijim posrednicima na razini književne kritike. Torbarina, Horvat, Krišković, Maraković i drugi... Drago mi je što sam izvukla na svjetlo dana neka imena koja su dosad bila marginalizirana ili potpuno potisnuta. Makar, čini mi se da rezultati toga posla od šest što ratnih što neratnih godina zvuče kao kreket žaba u bari? Jesmo li doista na repu svijeta? Povremeno me u tom uvjerenju poljulja događaj poput upada zadarskih *hackera* u kompjuterski sustav vojnih snaga SAD-a. Je li Pentagon bliži od neonom osvijetljenih knjižara uz Jelačić plac?

Posrednici. Mislim da bismo trebali biti svjesni uloge posrednika (kritičara, prevoditelja, kazališnog redatelja) a i samog čitatelja u recepciji književnine. Zapravo, na svijesti o čitateljevu "ispisivanju teksta čitanjem" temelji se cjelokupni algoritam postmodernističkog literarnog postupka. Inter-tekstualnost, alteritet, ironizacija, simultanizam...- izviru iz perspektive imaginarnog čitatelja. Pisac je pozvan tekstualno uobličiti predodžbe koje dobija simulirajući perspektivu recipijenta, receptivnu svijest. Ponekad svjesno na papiru trivijaliziram vlastitu emociju i književni čin. Ne stoga što mislim da sam tom činu nadređena. Naprotiv: bojim ga se. Kao što se bojim čitatelja. Zašto? Čitatelj je nadmoćan jer je obremenjen mogućnošću izbora. On ima Internet. Njegov je cijeli svijet. A moja je samo riječ. I ova ulica na Voštarnici. Veoma loše osvijetljena.

25. siječnja 1997.

Predvorje Filozofskog fakulteta. Profesor S. O., jedan od čelnih ljudi zadarskog ogranka Matice hrvatske zaustavlja me i podsjeća na dogovor u vezi sa zbirkom radova Studentskoga književnog kluba koji vodim od osnutka, od 1994. Od mene se očekuje da za knjigu koju kane objaviti odaberem tekstove i napišem predgovor. Teško da netko može zamisliti o kakvom se zapravo poslu radi: valja dešifrirati deset različitih pjesničkih svjetova. Još 1994. pripremila sam za objavljivanje knjigu članova Kluba, desetoro momaka i djevojaka, ali nitko (pa ni Fakultet na kojem oni studiraju) nije pokazao volju tiskati im knjižicu od sedamdesetak stranica. Možda ćemo sad imati više sreće. Klinci su ambiciozni, a što je najvažnije: među njima ima znatan broj nadarenih. Još će se za njih čuti.

27. siječnja 1997.

Prošloga je vikenda u Rim putovao "zadarski konvoj" sastavljen od četiri autobusa s predstavnicima Filozofskog fakulteta u Zadru, nadbiskupije i poglavarstva Grada Zadra. Time je, kažu, proslava zadarskih obljetnica - 600 godina od osnutka prvoga hrvatskog sveučilišta u sklopu Dominikanskog samostana i 40. godišnjica Filozofskog fakulteta - "dobila svoj epilog" (*Narodni list*). Tom je prigodom Papi uručena Krasićeva monografija o zadarskom generalnom učilištu. Mnogi me pitaju hoće li biti što od novog/obnovljenog zadarskog sveučilišta o kojemu se u posljednje vrijeme šuška. Je li izdaja lokalpatriotskih osjećaja odgovoriti pitanjem: može li se sveučilište graditi tamo gdje stanari jedinog studentskog doma žive bez grijanja i tople vode, gdje nema poštenog kina (a ovo postojeće nosi ime "Pobjeda"?!), gdje smo od početka kazališne sezone vidjeli tek dvije predstave, gdje nema Studentskoga kluba, gdje se mladež sastaje ili u mesingom opremljenim kafićima ili u bivšoj Gradskoj kavani pretrpanoj otpadom lansiranim pod etiketom "postmoder-nistički interijer"? Ili po uglovima ulica gdje se "žica" za još jedan *joint*. Ponudite im, gospodo, nešto u zamjenu za Novi Zeland!

2. veljače 1997.

Emin sedmi rođendan. Pravljenje kolača valja "utrpati" među ispite na Svjetskoj književnosti, peglanje hrpe odjeće, pisanje naručenih tekstova... Iznad štednjaka drag mi natpis: "Make lunch - not war!"[21]

3. veljače 1997.

Karneval - posebna priča. Već nekoliko godina u Zadru se od karnevala pravi - "karneval". Od sponzora u gospodarstvu, uprave Grada i Županije traži se novac za organiziranje pučke veselice s pimpekoidnim i cicoidnim gumenim maskama. Za potpun ugođaj na rimskom Forumu još nam samo Kaligula nedostaje. No, čini se da u narodu takva atavistička događanja "pale". Dajte da se veselimo pa makar tek dan (ili noć)! Dajte da pravimo majmune od sebe kad po cijele godine drugi prave majmune

[21] U doslovnom prijevodu: "Napravi ručak - ne rat!". To je parafraza glasovitoga gesla Djece cvijeća: „Make love – not war!" („Vodi ljubav a ne rat!").

od nas! Ali, naravno, ima ih koji i na ovome zarade lijepu paricu. Prošle je godine tako za tekst karnevalskog gradonačelnika i providura (Hej-haj autonomaši!) autor dobio više od po 5 tisuća kuna. Za par kartica teksta. Svaka čast. Treba znati uzeti. Kad ima. Skidam Vam kapu, autoru! A Vi, autoru, skinite masku!

17. veljače 1997.

Otputovala u Šibenik održati uvodno slovo na predstavljanju sasma friškog pretiska Zorčićeve *Vile dalmatinske* objavljene prvotno u Zadru prije 145 godina. Dakako, pretisak je izišao u nakladi vrijedne šibenske Gradske knjižnice "Juraj Šižgorić". Njihovim ljudima - Milivoju, Saši[22], Viliju... neugodno je slušati pohvale na račun njihova rada. "Poštedite nas tog govorničkog kiča!", kažu mi. Bože moj, znaju li ljudi koliko je truda potrebno da bi se objavile knjige u sredinama kao što su Šibenik i Zadar? "Priča o dva grada" ne završava posljednjom granatom u Domovinskom ratu; ona se nažalost nastavlja kroz na koljena bačeno gospodarstvo, kroz srozane umjetničke i uopće stvaralačke kriterije, kroz navodno "državotvorne" pjesničke večeri u kojima se stilistički vrhunac postiže uporabom aorista i imperfekta, kroz besramno veličanje i zahtijevanje domoljublja s govornica ispred kojih u prvim redovima sjede oni bez ruku, nogu ili vida. Znate li što u tom milieu znači tiskati knjige? Prisjećam se početaka i pokretanja *Glasja* još 1992. Obijali smo administrativne pragove i tražili sponzorske milodare za tiskanje časopisa dok nam je ponad glava zviždalo. Prisjećam se pripremanja mog scenskog kolaža "Kolega, rat predugo traje..." u ruševnoj zgradi Kazališta lutaka koje nam je kao dramskoj družini s fakulteta ustupilo prostor za probe i nastupe. U to doba, u svibnju 1995., bio je napadnut Zagreb. Tada je nastradao mali Luka, Zadranin. Knjige, predstave, radio emisije - grčevita, djetinjasta nada u mentalni i duševni opstanak. U ono doba binarnog sustava kad je bilo bitno tek ima li te ili te nema. Može li netko odvagati težinu tog posla, kojeg uostalom nismo držali poslom već egzistencijalnom potrebom?

19. veljače 1997.

Jutarnja kavica u kavani "Branimir" s imenjakinjom Helenom Roguljić, jedinim ženskim članom zadarskog ogranka DHK. Ona očekuje izlazak još jedne svoje pjesničke zbirke. Slučaj je htio da obje odaberemo istog zadarskog tiskara, sa simptomatičnim nazivom - GAFF. *Nomen est*

---

[22] Tek desetak dana po ovoj veceri Saša M., darovit i radin mladi ljubitelj književne rijeci otputovao je (većini znanaca i prijatelja nenajavljeno) s obitelji u Kanadu. Po svemu sudeći: da se više ovamo ne vrati. Barem ne kao hrvatski državljanin.

omen. Tiskanje moje zbirke *Pogledi (nešto kao...nametljivi zapisi)* potrajalo je kod njih više od godinu i pol. Helenina knjiga trebala je izići još pred dva mjeseca. "Profesionalizam" vlasnika tiskare skopčan je s (autorovim) ponižavajućim telefonskim pozivima i (tiskarovim) neutemeljenim obećanjima koja završavaju s "Uskoro..." Pretpostavljam da se to "uskoro" u mnogim slučajevima pretvori u "post mortem"... Komentiramo prošlogodišnju Izbornu skupštinu ogranka DHK u Zadru i odabir pedesetak ljudi od pera (ili novca!) za članove-suradnike. Farsa. Paravan za one koji znaju iskoristiti situaciju. Zadar postaje Meka za estradna literarno-komercijalna nadahnuća. Nazdravlje!

21. veljače 1997.

Listam *Narodni list* koji se i dalje "šverca" bez lektora. (Najstarije novine na Balkanu počet će zvučati kao istarsko-kvarnerska glasila. S prolupanom gramatikom i pravopisom.) U istom broju dva intervjua s dodirnom točkom: zadarskom Hrvatskom kazališnom kućom. Intervju s v.d. ravnateljicom HKK Verom Stipčević (ujedno i ravnateljicom zadarskoga Kazališta lutaka) i intervju sa zadarsko-(polu)paškim županom Prtenjačom. Previše se toga zakuhalo oko našega kazališta u posljednjih godinu dana.

23. veljače 1997.

Saznajem da Koncertni ured u Zadru priređuje nastup Zadarskog komornog orkestra i solista iz inozemstva. Svaka ovakva najava izazove moje grizodušje: kad god sretnem u gradu gospođu Branku D., poduzetnu voditeljicu Koncertnog ureda, posebno sentimentalnu prema ratnim pretplatnicima, moram joj se ispričavati što više ne posjećujem koncerte. Oni su se prestali održavati u predvorju kazališta jer se Ured odcijepio od HKK. Kako da Branki objasnim kako mi njihovi koncerti više ne predstavljaju "izlazak u život"? Ta oni sviraju tamo kamo ja odlazim na posao - na Filozofskom faksu. Uostalom, ja ne plešem kako/gdje drugi sviraju. Što, dakako, dodatno komplicira stvari.

24. veljače 1997.

Zbog Zorčića u Šibeniku propustila premijeru nove predstave Kazališta lutaka pod naslovom *San putujućeg glumca ili Princeza na zrnu graška*. Do dalnjeg predstava ide nedjeljom u dakako staroj zgradi, u Jazinama. Redatelj je predstave Bugar poznat pod pseudonimom Sunny Sunninsky. Od prošloga ljeta ovo mu je četvrta minijatura sa zadarskim lutkarima. Jedini glumac u ovoj predstavi je Zlatko Košta, nagrađivan kao najbolji hrvatski lutkar. Predstava je u stvari priznanje Zlatku. Zadrani su majstori lutkarstva. Takvi da se ovdje njihovo drugo mjesto na domaćim i međunarodnim natjecanjima drži porazom. A proći će još puno premijera dok se nova zgrada lutkarskog kazališta ne zgotovi. Najavljuju ovoga ljeta Carićevu adaptaciju *Planina*. Bojim se da će i to okončati kao većina njihovih "teških" predstava. Zašto barem minijature ne daju češće? Ta one se mogu prikazivati na trgovima.

Kad smjestite talent između siromaštva i megalomanije - što dobivate? Zadarski sendvič frustracije i malodušja.

28. veljače 1997.

Miriše na proljeće. Miriše na izbore. Što će biti sa Zadrom ove godine? Hoće li se uprave Grada i Županije prestati međusobno "gristi" i naći zajednički jezik? I hoće li "Jedan u kope - drugi u špade" prestati biti temeljnim načelom funkcioniranja (ne)kulture sjevernodalmatinskog Babilona? Čujem da se u sobama poglavarstva Grada Zadra gotovo svakodnevno baci po jedan telefon. I da se pritom dakako nešto i razbije: kakva kristalna pepeljara ili vaza. U gradu kojim vladaju kolerici trebalo bi naći mjesta za kulturu.

Čujem također da neki ljudi iz gradske i županijske uprave ne čitaju novine. I da im je mrsko obavljati poslove koji su izvan zadarskog Poluotoka (gdje inače rade i stanuju). Može li se to krstiti fobijom? A Poluotok je omeđen bedemima. Tu žive i kolo vode boduli. Koji u način života u Gradu usađuju mentalitet otočkih Robinzona - samodovoljnih, samodopadnih. Pa kako da ti kulturne vidike proširi i za njih stvori bolje uvjete u "vikendaškim" ustanovama - poput kina, kazališta, muzeja - onaj tko petkom hita na otok, među masline?

Sanjam o letu u svijet. Primjećujem čak da i moju Svjetsku književnost neki drže predmetom koji nije kompatibilan s turbo-nacionalnim duhom. Recite mi: kako da tumačim Držića bez Plauta i talijanske renesanse?

Možda pred ljeto, otputujemo u Španjolsku: Cristina i Judith očekuju nas već godinama. Bile su među onima - (a za takve je prevelik i broj prstiju jedne ruke) koji su u vihoru rata gotovo panično zvali da Ema dođe k njima. Možda su to oni zbog kojih sve ovo ima smisla. Rat je svakome bio teret. (Osim profiterima.) I možda je bespredmetno o njemu pričati onima koji ga nisu osjetili na način na koji te on pretvara u čovjeka od inata. Rat je bio prevelik gubitak vremena; donio je odviše gluposti da bi se danas mirili s hrpom apsurda. Ako kažem nekom u Zagrebu da mlada država jest dijete, ali dijete koje treba odgajati jer su djeca kvarljiva roba, onda me taj odmjeri i gotovo ljutito veli (ni ne sluteći koliko je uvredljivo to što kani reći) da je on "pravi domoljub". Ne znam, možda naše, provincijsko, ispodvelebitsko hrvatstvo valja mjeriti metrom planeta

Mars. Uostalom, pričati o ratnom iskustvu onima koji mu nisu opipali bilo znači izazivati u slušateljstvu nelagodu. To je kao da finim ljudima pričaš o lošoj probavi.

1. ožujka 1997.

Blažena veljača: kratko traje. Asistentska plaća kuca na vrata.

Svijet. I (Polu)otok.

U Zagrebu Zadar zovu "more" ili... "procvjetale bajame". A kako ću ga ja zvati ? "Tamo-gdje-dobijam-pisma-iz-svijeta".

17. srpnja 1997.

Paradiranje ili parodiranje? (*Narodni list*)

"O lijepa, o draga, o slatka slobodo..." - gromkim glasom naočiti glumac, gost iz Zagreba, recitira Gundulićevu "Dubravku" u vreloj srpanjskoj noći pred bijelim baldahinom što ga je skupina mladića i djevojaka razapela iznad svojih glava...

Ova će nas slika neminovno podsjetiti na otvaranje Dubrovačkih ljetnih igara, svetkovine kojom se veliča snaga i sloboda bijeloga utvrđenog grada na Jadranu. Ali ta se slika osim u Dubrovniku pred neku večer zgodila i u Zadru; u ponedjeljak je naime na našemu Narodnom trgu upriličeno svečano otvaranje prvoga zadarskog Kazališnog ljeta. U scenariju toga događaja bilo je udrobljeno štošta. Spomenimo neke momente ne nastojeći nužno slijediti izvorni redoslijed.

Svečanost je započela točkom ansambla za suvremeni ples temeljenoj na glazbi koja istodobno podsjeĆa na zbor cigana i Vandelisove beskrajne sintesajzerske etide. Glazbeni stilski obrat uslijedio je kada su Zadarski madrigalisti (dakako, u renesansnom ruhu) otpjevali Lijepu našu. Zatim je već spomenuti glumac iz Zagreba čitao nešto poput pozdravne riječi pokušavajući uporno odgonetnuti rukopis, da bi potom stao dozivati drugoga glumca-gosta (za kojeg se, da me ubiješ, nije moglo odgonetnuti je li trenutak ranije strusio koju čašicu ili popušio pošteni joint). Tako su se neko vrijeme ta dvojica natezali pa se nije znalo kane li se najavljeni glumci koji - kako nas ona dvojica upozoriše, nastupaju u ovoljetnim zadarskim komedijama - pojaviti u svjetlu reflektora ili ne. Zatim je zadarsko kninski "guverner", kako ga je naočiti voditelj svečanosti najavio, odao odu odavnim duhovnim patnjama Zadrana koji ni u ratnim nedaćama ne gube želju za kazalištem (posebice ako se ima na umu da u našemu gradu navike posjećivanja kazališnih predstava ne idu dalje od premijere!). Voditelj fešte opet je nešto pokušao razabrati na svojim papirićima i iako mu je glas gromak on bi jadničak povremeno i zamucnuo, što je imalo nemali groteskni učinak. Dok se on tako trudio iza njega prošli su na kamioncinu škovacini pobravši oduševljeni pljesak nazočnih. Pojedine su se scene u urednom neredu izmjenjivale uz vrijedne citate iz zadarske i ine hrvatske književne baštine: Barakovića, Zoranića, Preradovića, pa zera iz Milutina Cihlara Nehajeva. Sve to, tako lijepo isječeno, izmiješano i sklepano bilo je začinjeno nekim čudnim nametljivim neukusom (koji je na trenutke poprimao dimenzije blasfemije) temeljenom prije svega na činjenici da je gost-glumac, voditelj programa, za honorar koji će mu, pretpostavljam, biti isplaćen, u ponedjeljak oko 10 uvečer pod reflektorima prvi puta vidio svoj tekst.

Da je kojim slučajem gost iz Zagreba - koji nesumljivo zna zablistati u ulogama koje imaju *smisla* - imao čitati onaj nesretni tekst na otvorenju Ljetnih igara u Dubrovniku, možda bi uvaženi profesionalni glumac posvetio serviranom mu tekstu više profesionalne pozornosti (jer zna se što je Dubrovnik: tamo glumiše Hamleta D. Jacobi, D. Day Lewis i njima slični), ali čini se da je po sudu nekih za zadarsku publiku čak i ova nesretna improvizacija - med i mlijeko. Nespremnost i nespretnost u totalno rasklimanoj režiji, bolje rečeno, (nečijem privatnom) aranžmanu čitavoga otvorenja zadarskoga Kazališnog ljeta pretvorila se u krajnji bezobrazluk prema onima koji su prolaženje smetlarskog kamioncina iza pozornice shvatili kao u čitavom "spektaklu" jedine spontane i nadahnute trenutke - na sreću bila su dva (brojkom: 2) i to u smjeru "tamo i vamo"! Vjerujem da su i ti autentični trenuci koji su izazvali oduševljenje u gledalištu bili pošteno sponzorirani.

Zadarska publika kojoj se povremeno u kazališnom celofanu ne prodaju bubrezi već nešto sasvim drugo - i ne očekuje više. Tako izgleda razmišljaju dušobrižnici iz naše Kazališne kuće. Ili je možda jedino važno da se u gradu "nešto događa"? Uvjerena sam da bi bilo bolje da se umjesto ovakvih "nešto" ne događa ništa: jeftine (a za neke možda i unosne) svetkovine intonirane imperativnim domoljubljem nisu ono čime je običnog čovjeka s ratom na leđima uljudno šopati. Ima li netko silnu želju da zadarsko Kazališno ljeto učini tradicionalnim bilo bi silno zgodno da od ovakvih "trijumfalnih" otvaranja Ljeta ne čini tradiciju.

Ako je točno da su u pripremi ovoga čuda, u koje su utkani često zlorabljeni stihovi "Zora puca - bit će dana", sudjelovali nama poznati zadarski kazalištarci onda ja njih - ne u ulozi kritičara, već gledatelja - iskreno pitam: Što je vama i nama to trebalo?

Dakle, pedeset godina nakon osnutka zadarskoga Hrvatskog narodnog kazališta (ta se naime činjenica spominje na plakatima za Kazališno ljeto) zora je pukla, ali čini se za nekog tko ju je zlorabio za polupijano paradiranje i parodiranje otvaranja Dubrovačkih igara (i to) na središnjem zadarskom trgu.

Zora puče. A dan?

13. rujna 1997.

Moj se život prije svršetka dvaput sklopi
Još ostaje vidjeti
Hoće li Besmrtnost treći događaj
Meni razotkriti - - - [23]

San

Na pola našeg životnoga puta...[24] U dobi od tridesetpet godina... Stojim na vrhu brda. Među oblacima i vjetrom. Iz podnožja brda izviru., jedan po jedan. Koračaju lagano, gotovo lebdeći, suzbijajući silu težu i sve druge fizikalne zakone. Čak im ni snažno jugo ne smeta. Strepim da će se okrenuti i otići. No, oni se i dalje približavaju ne zastajući, ne kolebajući se; prozračni, blijedih lica i vodenastih očiju s naglašeno crvenim rubovima kapaka. Kao u staraca. Ne znam tko su oni uistinu (teško ih je prepoznati iz veće udaljenosti). Vjetar i kapi kiše - rijetke ali velike i teške - šibali su im lica: kosa je vijorila a vlažna se odjeća pripila uz tijelo.

Prvi mi se primakao Niko. On je najsvježiji među njima. Valjda zato što im se zadnji pridružio. Lice mu se najjasnije vidi. S velikim dalekovidnim dioptrijama u pozlaćenim metalnim okvirima, skakuće, pocupkuje - onako s trbuščićem - veselo kao uvijek. Pod jednim pazuhom nosi bačvicu najboljeg belgijskog piva (koje nismo stigli kušati). Pod drugim mu je svežanj fotografija. Pristupio mi je razdragano a onda pogledao ravno u oči. U tom trenu nesta mu osmijeha s lica, bačvica se otkotrlja nizbrdo a fotografije raspu i razlete na vjetru. Bile su uglavnom crno-bijele. Vjerovao je da boja oduzima dostojanstvo fotografijama: da afektira u situaciji kada svako afektiranje znači zapravo bogohuljenje. Bile su to snimke s rock-koncerata, s političkih sjednica, snimke cvijeća, križeva, pušaka, majki s rupcem na glavi, djece zgrčena lica. Jedina fotografija u boji prikazivala je njegovu ženu i kćer; one neobično nalikuju jedna drugoj - imaju duge trepavice na zelenosmeđim očima pravilna oblika, poput ploda slatkaste dalmatinske čičindre.

---

[23] Iz jedne pjesme američke pjesnikinje Emily Dickinson. Prevela H. P.

[24] Početni stih Danteova *Pakla*.

Niku slijedi kolona u kojoj su: Snježanin brat, neosporni dar za matematiku i fiziku, moja Silvana, pa Ladina sestra, pa mali Luka, koji je trebao biti veliki redatelj, Chester Beers - vijetnamski veteran i pjesnik, pa Tanjin sedamnaestogodišnji nećak Neven, pa mladić - sin jednoga kolege - koji je prije par godina, kažu, u pijanu stanju provirio glavom kroz tramvajski prozor, pa brat kolegice s filozofije kojega su upucali dok je u uniformi hrvatskoga vojnika bio u nekom splitskom kafiću, oslijepljeni dječa iz Srebrenice, djevojčica Irma iz Sarajeva, pa vojnici iz Sukošana, mahom vršnjaci mojega brata, koji su nastradali pokraj Škabrnje... One koji su mi bili dragi, ili one koje sam tek površno poznavala, ili one o kojima sam čitala u novinama a opet bliski ljudima s kojima sam radila, družila se, prijateljevala... - sve sam ih prepoznala, makar nekima ni imena znam. I svi oni poskakuju poput balerina, vedra lica, bez ožiljaka, pošteđeni posljedica tuđeg ili vlastitog nasilja nad svojim tijelom. Kad su mi se konačno svi približili, spustili su na tlo sve ono što su nosili - sljepačke štapove, puške, logaritamske tablice, kamere, lijekove, bombe - uhvatili se za ruke i okružili me, kao u kolu, plešući, hihočući se, ulazeći i izlazeći iz oblaka i vjetra... *Danse macabre - danse macabre - danse ma-ca-bre...* Puhalo je nemilo. Već se smračilo i noć su presijecali bljeskovi munje. Zemlja se močila i osjećala sam svaki grumen kako po tlu poskakuje pod silinom velikih kapi kiše. Pitah se: kako vam je pod zemljom, kako vam je u ovoj vjetrovitoj i kišnoj noći, kako na svojim položenim tijelima podnosite težinu ovog neba.

17. studenog 1997.

Dragi Petre[25],

pretpostavljam da će te iznenaditi ovo pismo jer ti odavna nisam pisala i zasigurno si povjerovao da ti više neću ni pisati.

Jedan od razloga zašto ne pisah - a vjerujem da ga kao takvog nećeš prihvatiti - jest taj da pisanje pisama nekome tko je daleko od ove učmale, ubojite, marinkovićevske sredine apsolutno nema smisla. Svako naklapanje autora pisma o bijedi - i duhovnoj i onoj za koju kažu da nije bitna (a to kažu oni koji materijalnu bijedu nikada okušali nisu) - ponižava i autora pisma i onoga tko pismo čita.

Čemu pisati nekome tko se nalazi tako daleko od svega ovoga? Naprosto: zanijemim od te silne udaljenosti do Švicarske (*Emily Dickinson...*), od te (možda prividne ali ipak doživljajne) "čistoće" kojom si ti okružen a koju se ja usuđujem nagrizati svojim mizernim slavenskim frustracijama, svojom agresivnom (pred)balkanskom inferiornošću i tisućljetnim poludivljaštvom.

---

[25] Ovaj je Petar ista osoba kao u „17. travnja 1996.".

Ova je godina proletjela kao u snu i čini mi se da su siječanj i obrana doktorata bili jučer. Ljeto je "iscurilo" u raščiščavanju otpada u staroj kući Darkovoga djeda u Petrčanima u kojoj se nije živjelo barem četvrt stoljeća, koja je vlažna, građena očito bez pravih temelja, i krcata trulim i nepotrebnim stvarima koje je u nju Darkov otac desetljećima trpao.

Skoro će ponoć i Ema spava pokraj mene nakon dana u kome je dugo sa mnom razgovarala o svom tati. Pored ovih sitnih a ogromnih emocionalno-egzistencijalnih problema svoje 7,9 godina stare kćeri utopljena sam u komešanja unutar svoje obitelji (odnosi s roditeljima, bratom...) s metalnim okusom unaprijed izgubljenih protupatrijarhalnih okršaja povišena tona u kvaziintelektualnim, površnim i ponižavajućim raspravama.

Zagreb je bio i ostao dalek. U stvari, postaje sve udaljeniji. U Zadru već mjesecima nije bilo kazališne predstave a koncert se zgodi - ako Bog da - jednom u mjesec i po dana (a kad se i zgodi ja ga ne posjetim jer se održava u zgradi Filozofskog fakulteta: ne da mi se ići na koncerte tamo gdje radim).

Nije lako odlučiti se živjeti ovdje.

Ema je izrasla u prekrasno djevojče velikih očiju i radosna srca (ili barem silne želje za radosnim srcem). Dajem joj ljubavi koliko mogu, istiskujući posljednji atom energije svoga skoliotičnoga tijela uništena sjedenjem, tipkanjem, mozganjem... Svake večeri liježem pored nje dok ne usne. I to mi je naslađi dio dana/večeri. Leći kraj te čiste a ogromne dječje duše.

Bilo bi lijepo da nam se javiš.

Srdačno te pozdravljam.

Helena

17. siječnja 1998.

Na sjednici Odsjeka, stariji kolega jezikoslovac sjeo za stol meni nasuprot i prostro pred sobom moje članke izrezane iz *Vijenca* te moj intervju iz novogodišnjeg broja *Zadarskoga lista*. Kolega se očito dobro pripremio za ovaj sastanak i ozbiljno odlučio govoriti o mojim tekstovima i izjavama vezanim uz status predmeta Svjetska književnost u okviru zadarskoga studija kroatistike. No, sva sreća da se sastanak odužio, pa je kolega bio prisiljen nekamo otići prije no što je stigao red na njega. Prije par mjeseci otvoreno mi je na ulici (pokraj Sv. Šime, iako se predstavlja kao veliki katolik!) predložio da on (kao jezikoslovac!) i još i dvojica profesora - ugledni stručnjak pred mirovinom tužna lica a vesela srca, te gostujući profesor, dramski autor s nizom izvora redovitih mjesečnih prihoda (sve redom kroatisti - a nitko od njih komparatist!) formiraju

Komisiju (sic!) koja će odrediti program i literaturu za moj predmet - Svjetska književnost.

\- - -
Mi nikada nećemo popiti bruderšaft
niti se naslađivati
u medijima nezabilježenom polemikom

Bez znanstvene aparature, kolega,
zaključujem: nisam mito-man (mea culpa)
i ne pišem u desetercu (mea maxima culpa)

I - ni Vi ni ja nemamo vremena za
isuviše malu razliku
između idiotarija i maksima

I ne dopuštam da me učite
Hrvatsku voljeti
Hrvatsku mrziti

(Jer) postojani me podučiše nepostojanosti
sjedeći u zadnjem redu
vlastite principijelnosti (jeftina sjedišta)- - - [26]

EPILOG (1999.):

1. Brat Snježane T. - ubio se tako da je sebi pucao u glavu iz očeva pištolja u rujnu 1991. - na početku svega ovoga.
2. Sin kolege M. S. - smrtno stradao vozeći se tramvajem u Zagrebu 1993.
3. Jesen 1993. u Zadru - obilovala samoubojstvima.
4. Sestra Lade S.- ubila se u proljeće 1994. bacivši se s neke zgrade na Voštarnici.
5. Unuk bivšeg pukovnika JNA ubio se aktivirajući bombe koje je nosio oko pojasa. Dogodilo se to u vrijeme velikog odmora u učionici Tehničke škole, u studenom 1994.
6. Sin kolege V. S. - Luka, daroviti student režije na zagrebačkoj Akademiji, nakon mjesec dana podlegao ranama zadobivenim u bombardiranju Zagreba u svibnju 1995.

---

[26] Iz moje pjesme *Kolega, rat predugo traje...*

7. Pokćerka i zet (i zetov brat) profesora A. F. smrtno nastradali 1995. u prometnoj nesreći; za jednu od preživjelih djevojčica ne zna se hoće li ikada moći samostalno hodati.

8. Brat-blizanac moje kolegice T. G. H. ubio se 2. veljače 1995. u Skopju.

9. Nikša Antonini, fotoreporter i moj prijatelj, poginuo 3. travnja 1996. u avionskoj nesreći: američki vojni avion u kojem se vozila političko-gospodarska delegacija SAD iz Tuzle u Dubrovnik, udario je u brdo Sv. Ivan ponad Konavala. Do danas njegovoj supruzi nije plaćena odšteta.

10. Točno četiri mjeseca nakon Nikšine smrti, 3. kolovoza 1996. moja sestrična izvršila samoubojstvo bacivši se sa šestog kata. Bile su joj 44 godine.

11. Od početka 1999. do sredine srpnja iste godine na zadarskom području izvršeno dvadesetšest (brojkom: 26) samoubojstava. Polovicu izvršitelja čine dragovoljci Domovinskog rata.

\- - -
Kiši... i jesen je... i rat je ... i Hrvatska
i nije mi do prežvakavanja
u podlistku lokalnih novina- - - [27]

* * *

Rekoh: Kad sve ovo završi nipošto neću imati vremena za svoje gluposti i tuđe svinjarije.

I rekoh: Mojim bližnjima - Petru i Pavlu - ovo nešto vrijedi. Ima li još koji svetac na mojoj strani?

---

[27] Nastavak prethodno započetog zapisa

APPENDIX

Map 1

Map of Croatia. Retrieved from www.cia.gov/library/publications/the-world-factbook/geos/

Map 2

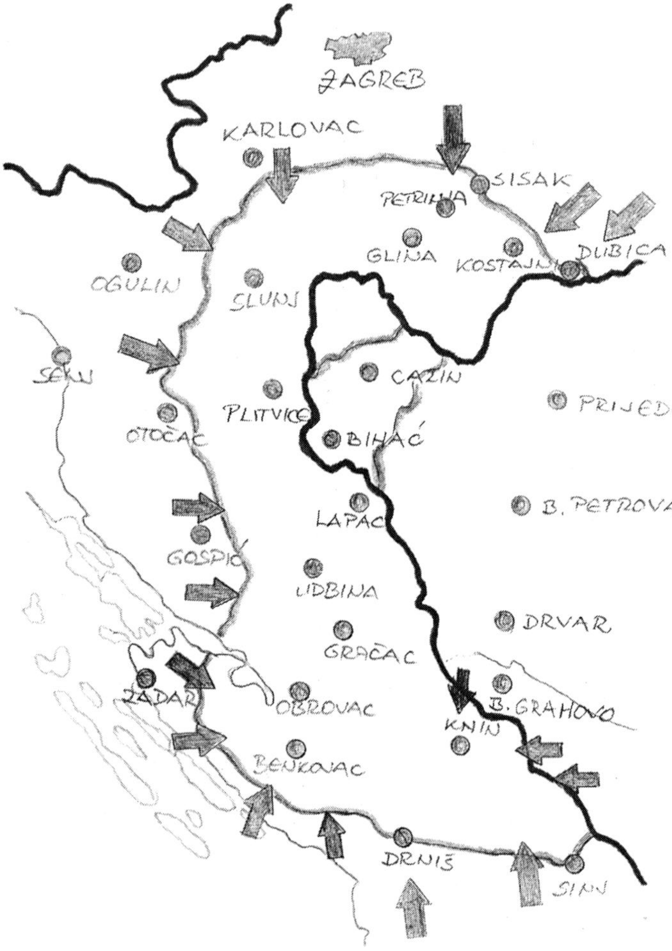

The area within the arrows on the map is the region of central Croatia occupied by the enemy army (most of which remained occupied until August 1995); an authentic map from the Homeland War. Courtesy of UDVDR RH – Zadar / Association of Homeland War Volunteers and Veterans of Republic Croatia, Zadar Branch.

Postcards from Zadar (autumn 1991)

“B. Bersa” School of Music. Design: Igor Gluić; photo by: Željko Karavida. Publisher: Independent Squad of Artists from Zadar.

Zadar, Autumn 1991. Design: Igor Gluić; photo by: Arif Ključanin. Publisher: Independent Squad of Artists from Zadar.